THE ART OF
PUTTING

THE ART OF
PUTTING

···

The Revolutionary Feel-Based System
for Improving Your Score

Stan Utley
with Matthew Rudy

GOTHAM
BOOKS

GOTHAM BOOKS
Published by Penguin Group (USA) Inc.
375 Hudson Street, New York, New York 10014, U.S.A.
Penguin Group (Canada), 90 Eglinton Avenue East, Suite 700, Toronto, Ontario, M4P
2Y3, Canada (a division of Pearson Penguin Canada Inc.); Penguin Books Ltd, 80
Strand, London WC2R 0RL, England; Penguin Ireland, 25 St Stephen's Green, Dublin
2, Ireland (a division of Penguin Books Ltd); Penguin Group (Australia), 250
Camberwell Road, Camberwell, Victoria 3124, Australia (a division of Pearson Australia
Group Pty Ltd); Penguin Books India Pvt Ltd, 11 Community Centre, Panchsheel Park,
New Delhi – 110 017, India; Penguin Group (NZ), cnr Airborne and Rosedale Roads,
Albany, Auckland 1310, New Zealand (a division of Pearson New Zealand Ltd);
Penguin Books (South Africa) (Pty) Ltd, 24 Sturdee Avenue, Rosebank, Johannesburg
2196, South Africa

Penguin Books Ltd, Registered Offices: 80 Strand, London WC2R 0RL, England

Published by Gotham Books, a division of Penguin Group (USA) Inc.

First printing, May 2006
10 9 8 7 6 5 4 3 2 1

LIBRARY OF CONGRESS CATALOGING-IN-PUBLICATION DATA
Utley, Stan.
    The art of putting : the revolutionary feel-based system for improving your score /
Stan Utley with Matt Rudy.
        p. cm.
    ISBN 1-59240-202-X (hardcover)
    1. Putting (Golf)   I. Rudy, Matthew.   II. Title.
    GV979.P8U87 2006
    796.352'35—dc22   2005035695

Printed in the United States of America
Set in Augustal
Designed by Kathryn Parise

While the author has made every effort to provide accurate telephone numbers and
Internet addresses at the time of publication, neither the publisher nor the author
assumes any responsibility for errors, or for changes that occur after publication.
Further, the publisher does not have any control over and does not assume any
responsibility for author or third-party websites or their content.

CONTENTS

· ·

FOREWORD
by Jay Haas

Nine-time winner on the PGA Tour and three-time
Ryder Cup team member

. . . .

You might be wondering if Stan Utley can really help you fix the problems you're having with your putter. I can tell you first hand that it's true.

Stan and I were casual acquaintances from the years we were both playing on the tour in the 1980s and 1990s, and I certainly knew about Stan's wonderful touch with his own putter. I had even heard through the grapevine that he was really helping some other guys on tour with their putting and chipping. But I didn't really get to know Stan until April 2001, just after I had gone through an absolutely miserable season with my putter. At forty-eight years old, I was at the point where I was trying to figure out how to hang on out on tour at least until I could play the Champions Tour starting in 2004.

Stan happened to be having dinner at my brother-in-law Dillard Pruitt's house in Greenville, South Carolina, my hometown, when I came by. We started talking about putting and I told him my story. I was expecting to set up a lesson or something on the practice green later that week, but Stan took me outside that night to look at my stroke under the porch light. I made a change to my grip after hearing what he had to say, and started to practice the stroke he teaches. Every two weeks or so, we'd talk on the phone about my putting stroke. The week we finally got together and had an "official lesson," in Milwaukee, I made nine birdies the next day. Then I finished second the following week.

I know it sounds like a cliché to say that some kind of light clicked on in my head after talking to Stan, but it really did. I felt so much better over my putts, and I immediately began to see positive things start to happen during tournament rounds. In my second event of the 2003 season, I shot 61 on Friday at the Bob Hope and went on to finish second. I don't care what tour you're playing on—when you go 11-under for the day and 28-under for the week, it makes you feel pretty good about how you're rolling the ball.

We've got all kinds of statistics measuring what we do week in and week out here on the PGA Tour. Heck, you can even find out what percentage of six-footers you're making for the season with the click of a mouse. But for me, there's an easy way to confirm just how much Stan has helped me over the last few years. I'm swinging as well—or even better—than I did when I was twenty-five or thirty-five. I'm hitting the ball longer than ever, too. But in 1992, I was ninety-eighth on the money list, and the year before I was ninety-second, hitting the ball just like I am now. After working with Stan on my putting, I had eight top-ten finishes in 2003 and earned $2.6 million. Now, at age fifty-two, I'm lucky enough to be able to pick and choose what senior events I play because I'm still competitive on the PGA Tour. Stan's been a big part of that success.

The first thing Stan will tell anybody—from a tour player like me to the average amateur—is that he isn't a miracle worker. But that's the beauty of what he teaches. There aren't any gimmicks or complicated techniques that you have to worry about holding up under pressure. He's teaching solid, basic fundamentals in the putting game that match up with the basic fundamentals of a good full swing. Anybody can learn them, and anybody can putt better using them—whether that means shooting a 61, like I did, or feeling more confident over that ten-footer you've got to break ninety for the first time.

Jay Haas
Greenville, SC
December 1, 2005

INTRODUCTION

· ·

Let me tell you about a typical putting lesson I give here at Gray-hawk Golf Club in Scottsdale, Arizona, where I teach when I am home. First, I always clarify two things: One, because I am a player, I emphasize that shooting low is the No. 1 goal, even ahead of great fundamentals; two, if you're looking to get better, I'll always do my best to help you improve with the fundamentals I believe and trust.

Now we are ready to get to work. I always ask a number of questions to learn a player's thoughts about putting, and then have him or her hit a few putts. When I'm teaching somebody for the first time, I can often literally see the tension radiating from the player's body—from the anxious expression on the person's face to the fact that you can see the neck start to disappear as the shoulders pull in and get tight.

But putting doesn't have to stress you out that way. Trust me. I know it's hard to believe, especially after *another* three-putt, or when you miss the hole on a five-footer that would have won you ten bucks from your buddies.

What if I told you that learning a few simple fundamentals about the putting stroke and grip could loosen those shoulders and take away most of that anxiety? My goal with this book is to help you make your putting skill more accurately reflect your talent level. And the good news is, haven't seen a single person who didn't have enough natural feel and athletic ability to be at least a decent putter. *Not one.*

Putting well doesn't have anything to do with how big or small you are, how far you can hit your driver, or even what your handicap is. If you can incorporate some of the fundamentals I teach into your stroke, you can become a more accurate putter. Does that mean you're going to go out and one-putt eighteen greens during your round tomorrow? Probably not. The best I've managed to do myself is twenty-one, at the 2002 Bell Canadian Open. But I'm sure you'll agree that building a more consistent, repeatable stroke and developing a better feel for break and distance is going to help you make more putts and leave your misses closer to the hole. If you're three-putting seven or eight times in a round right now, I can help you turn your ninety-five round into an eighty-seven or eighty-eight.

In *The Art of Putting*, I'm going to share with you the putting fundamentals and secrets I learned though years of study on the PGA Tour and refined through hundreds of hours of short-game lessons given to players like Jay Haas, Peter Jacobsen and Darren Clarke. In the first chapter, I'll take you back to the beginning of my golf career and describe my introduction to the fundamentals of putting—the foundation of the almost thirty years of success I've had on the putting green. Chapter 2 covers the basics, from the grip to setup and posture. In Chapter 3, I'll help you pick the right kind of putter for your stroke, and show you how important it is to have that putter fit to your body. Chapters 4 and 5 are really what I consider to be the heart of this instruction book. In Chapter 4, I'll give you a step-by-step guide to making a good putting stroke—and show you how I do it with a high-speed photo sequence. Chapters 5 and 6 cover the psychology of putting and some of the more advance skills and strategies you need on the putting green, from green reading to lag putting.

I'm extremely fortunate to have been able to work with a variety of talented tour players, and honored that they would trust me to help them with their games. In Chapter 7, I'll tell you about some of the things that Jay Haas, Craig Stadler, Peter Jacobsen, Rocco Mediate and Darren Clarke have worked on in their own putting games, and I'll show you some of the other common faults that can creep into a putting stroke and how to fix them. In Chapter 8, I'll take you through a series of drills that will get your putting stroke in shape and keep it there all season. The last chapter, a quick reference guide, is designed to help you quickly diagnose your own putting problems and to use the concepts I teach to make instant corrections.

Good luck, and good putting.

CHAPTER 1
WHAT DO I KNOW?

· ·

What do *I* know, and why should you listen to me about your putting stroke? Good questions. Let me try to answer them for you.

I don't have the greatest record as a PGA Tour player. I'm proud of the fact that I won out there, at the 1989 Chattanooga Classic, but they aren't clearing out any space for my memorabilia at the World Golf Hall of Fame. I'm also not in the same league as guys like David Leadbetter or Butch Harmon when it comes to fixing full-swing problems for tour players hoping to win major championships.

But when it comes to the short game—putting, chipping and sand play—I've been blessed with a special combination of skills and training. I've been a good putter since I was a little kid, and I got great instruction on how to take advantage of those skills from Ken Lanning, one of the legendary teachers in my home state of Missouri. My putting and short game have made it possible for a guy who can't hit it 300 yards and who doesn't hit more than nine or ten greens per round to make a living on the PGA Tour.

There are certainly other tour players out there who can really roll the ball. But I'm lucky enough to be able to roll my ball better than most *and* explain to you how you can get yours to roll better, too. I haven't seen too many other teachers who can say they've done it at the highest level and can help other players understand it, too. I'm still playing on the PGA and Nationwide Tours, but more and more of my time goes to helping tour players like Jay Haas, Peter Jacobsen, Darren Clarke and up and coming pros and juniors— and average amateurs as well—get better on and around the green. Believe it or not, the teaching part got started almost by accident.

When I first turned pro, the prize money wasn't anywhere near what it is today. That meant lots of carpooling, sharing hotel rooms, and cheap takeout food with other guys playing in the same mini-tour events. I spent hours talking golf with guys like Brandel Chamblee, and Willie Wood. Brandel was always working on his swing—talking about it, reading books, watching videos. I had a knack for putting and the short game, so I'd share some of what I learned, and Brandel would give me something to use on my full swing. What I was telling Brandel back in 1985 wasn't much different than what I say today—and it's fundamentally the same thing I first heard from Ken Lanning, back when I was in middle school. Without Mr. Lanning, I wouldn't be where I am today.

I didn't really start out as a golfer. My dad was a tremendous athlete who chose to go to work on the railroad and start a family instead of going to college and playing sports. So when my brother and I came along, he introduced us at an early age to basketball, football and baseball, the sports he played in industrial leagues in my hometown of Thayer, Missouri. My dad still tells the story about sneaking retired major league pitcher Preacher Roe—who lived down the street from us in West Plains—into a rec baseball game to throw a few innings with my dad as his battery mate.

My dad is a tremendous teacher of kids, and right from the beginning, I had an advantage because he taught me what I was supposed to do when I had the ball. I wasn't the fastest kid or the highest jumper, but I was the point guard on the basketball team and the quarterback on the football team. Basketball was my life, but a funny thing happened in junior high school. By the time I was fourteen years old, I was pretty much full grown. At that point, I figured out that I wasn't going to be the next Walt Frazier or Dr. J., and golf came around at just the right time in my life.

I was first introduced to golf when I was ten years old. One of my dad's friends gave me an old black-faced MacGregor 3-iron, and I used to knock balls around the yard on our farm in Thayer. Before I started the sixth grade, my parents moved us thirty miles down the road, from Thayer to West Plains. West Plains had a bigger school system than Thayer, and it had a nine-hole golf course, too. We were three blocks from West Plains Country Club, and it didn't take me long to get hooked.

The junior clinics at West Plains were run by a woman named Rhoda Luna, who played in the men's matches from the back tees when she wasn't showing us kids where to stand and how to hold it. I seemed to have the knack for it right from the start. I liked all the freedom to play the hole any way you wanted. I loved golf for the same reason then as I do now: I didn't have to rely on anybody else to make the right decision with the ball for it to turn out the way I wanted. When things went good, I knew I was the one who had hit the shots.

When I was thirteen, my dad and I were playing in a scramble tournament and we were paired with Mr. Lanning, who was famous in southern Missouri as a teacher and a player. One of my first golf memories is from that day, when Mr. Lanning told my dad that if I was serious about golf, he would help me. Mr. Lanning's interest seemed to show my dad that I had some real potential, and he agreed to drive me the hundred miles to Mr. Lanning's club to get lessons every month.

You're going to read a lot about the putting basics in the next few chapters, and you can thank Mr. Lanning for that. He was a stickler for the basics, and he believed that if you made the game simple and kept to a few simple principles, you'd play your best golf. He worked with me on my full swing more than anything else early on, and I got to playing really well. When I was in ninth grade, I was already playing on the high school team—even though I was in my last year of middle school. I wouldn't call myself a superstar in high school golf, but I got better every year. By my senior year, I was averaging right around par on southern Missouri's country-club courses.

When it came time to think about college, I was considering places that were consistent with my Christian faith—like Harding College in Arkansas and David Lipscombe in Nashville. I wasn't really thinking about Division I golf, but Rich Poe at the University of Missouri recruited me and offered me a little scholarship. It was a chance to save my parents some money, so I drove 200 miles north to Columbia to go to school at Mizzou.

The best part about Missouri was that the team wasn't that good and Coach Poe had a great relationship with a lot of the other golf coaches. The lineup wasn't so strong that a freshman like me couldn't make the traveling team, and we got to bump heads with teams like Oklahoma State, Texas and Houston on a regular basis. In fact, I tell high school golfers all the time that it's not a bad idea to go to a college where you can play a lot, because it's the only way to find out if you can really compete at the top level.

I got to find out right away, because our conference was loaded. Steve Jones was at Colorado, and Oklahoma had Andrew Magee and Greg Turner. Willie Wood was playing at Oklahoma State, and Scott Verplank would get there my senior year. Houston had a whole bunch of guys who eventually went pro—Billy Ray Brown and Steve Elkington—and Brandel Chamblee and Mark Brooks were at Texas. We didn't play any of the good West Coast teams, but we played in some competitive, top-flight tournaments.

In my sophomore year, I finished in the top ten at the conference tournament, which was both a good and bad thing. It was great to know that I could compete with some of the best college players in the world, but I could definitely see that there were guys who could do things with a golf ball that I couldn't do. Ever since high school, my goal was to be a tour player. For the first time, I realized it wasn't going to be so easy.

Before my junior year, Mr. Lanning sat me down and told me that

I was a good putter, but that I really needed to learn the mechanics of the putting stroke both to improve my stroke and be able to understand what to do when my stroke was off. I spent that whole summer going over Mr. Lanning's complete checklist of basics—stance, setup, grip—the things I'm going to show you in the pages of this book. You could compare pictures of my putting stroke after that summer of work with the way I putt now and they'd be identical. The method is simple and solid, and I've never had any reason to change it. I'm lucky and grateful to have gotten such an in-depth education in the art of putting at such an early age. It's the same stuff I'm now teaching every day to players of all levels.

My game took a big step forward in my junior year. I was named second-team All-America, and seeing my name on that plaque, with a lot of guys who are still earning their living playing golf today, was a proud moment in my life. I was also starting to shoot some of the low scores you need to compete at the top level of the game. I finished second in the conference tournament in my junior year, to Andrew Magee, and second again in my senior year, to Scott Verplank. The guys who were beating me were serious, talented, tour-ready guys, so I felt like I had a chance to make a living at the game. We won the conference tournament as a team my senior year—the first time Missouri had ever won it, and the first time in forever Oklahoma State hadn't won it. I knew I wanted to try pro golf, but we didn't have the money as a family for me to get some kind of bankroll for a year on the road. So I hung out in Missouri that summer, playing in some local tournaments, and traveled to the U.S. Amateur at Oak Tree, in Edmond, Oklahoma. I lost in the quarterfinals there, then turned professional just in time to go back to school in the fall to finish my degree. I would have to try to make it in pro golf in my free time.

A couple of my buddies were going over to Jackson, Mississippi, to play in a little pro event, so I went along, too. I paid my entry fee, teed it up and won the darn thing. I collected my $750 check and drove back home. The next week, my college coach was playing in a big PGA sectional club pro event, the Southern Illinois Open. I'm sure they weren't so happy to see a college kid tagging along, but I went out and won that one, too. I can remember driving back with $2,000 in my pocket, thinking to myself, "Hey, this is the life. It doesn't get any easier than this." Of course, I'd find out pretty quick that that wasn't exactly true.

Once I graduated in December, I figured it was time to go out and give it a try for real. My dad went down to the bank and signed for a line of credit, and I signed a note with him. He gave me an old Oldsmobile Toronado to drive, and I shook his hand and went out to try to make my way. I started knocking around the mini-tours in Arizona and Texas, playing terrible and losing money every week. I was lucky enough to get a sponsor—a doctor from Houston who was a friend of one of my dad's friends—and that took a tremendous amount of pressure off me. I could concentrate on my golf game instead of wondering how I was going to pay my bills at the end of the month. With a little financial breathing room, my wife Elayna and I were able to get married in 1987. It was just the two of us, our $300-a-month apartment in Columbia and my old car.

The money supply wasn't endless, so I fell into a routine of playing mini-tour events that were reasonable drives from home, along with a circuit of state opens in Missouri and the surrounding states. I was treading water, making a little money here and there, but nothing much was happening for me. I have to give Elayna all the credit in the world, because at the end of the 1988 season, she laid down the law. She told me I had a bad attitude and wasn't getting good results, so I had to try something different if I was going to keep going out there and spending the money to travel and enter these tournaments.

So I went back to see Coach Poe at Missouri, and I asked him if he knew of any sports psychologists who could help me with the mental side of my game. Not only did he know somebody, he knew somebody who was right there on campus. It turned out that Rick McGuire, the Missouri track coach, was one of the most prominent sports psychologists in the world. He worked in the psychology department and coached Olympic track athletes. Dr. McGuire introduced me to one of his colleagues, Dr. David Cook, who was into golf, and David and I hit it off right away. We started working together in 1989, and I soon began to see some improvement, at least in the consistency of my mental routine.

Rick, David and I got together for a "mental summit meeting" the week of the Kansas Open that summer, and David gave me a complete routine to use to focus my concentration on the course—which basically involved visualizing my shots, feeling what was necessary to hit them and then trusting it and letting it go. I decided to pitch all of my mechanical swing thoughts and just go with the mental process David designed and see where it got me. I plugged it in and finished in the top five in Kansas. The next week, David played with me in the pro-am at the Missouri Open and got me locked in. I shot 17-under and won the tournament. The first-place check was $10,000—which allowed me to pay back a loan from a friend and clear all my other debt. I was even with the world, and I had a sponsor's exemption into the PGA Tour event the next week in Chattanooga. My life was about to change forever.

The tournament organizers in Chattanooga had given me an exemption into the event because I had qualified the year before and shot the low round of the day on Sunday. I was obviously feeling pretty good about my game coming off a win at the Missouri Open, and I was looking forward to trying Dave Cook's focusing techniques on a bigger stage.

We finished up our third round Sunday morning, and I ended up shooting 6-under to get into the last group with John Daly, who was also playing on a sponsor's exemption. John was four or five shots ahead of me at the start of the round, but he struggled a little bit and I made some birdies to get back into it. The only thing I'm thinking about is Dave Cook's mental checklist—see it, feel it, trust it—and all of a sudden, I'm in the lead on the tenth hole.

We got to seventeen, a short par-5, and I knew that Ray Stewart had just finished and was a shot ahead of me. I missed my tee shot in what was the standard place for me at the time, the left trees, and was looking at some sort of 7-iron layup shot. As I pulled the club, my caddie, Hawk, got in front of me and told me that you don't win golf tournaments by laying up on reachable par-5. For some reason, I listened to him and sliced a 3-wood over the trees and onto the middle of the green. I had a fifty- or sixty-footer for eagle and eased it up to a foot for a tap-in birdie.

The eighteenth hole was a big dogleg, and I can remember being so into my process—see it, feel it, trust it—that I didn't even notice what anybody else was doing. I hit my 3-wood right down the middle, hit a 5-iron to fifteen feet and pured that putt right in the center of the cup. All of a sudden, I was a winner on the PGA Tour, and I had a two-year exemption. I would be in the field in Milwaukee on Thursday and I didn't even know where Milwaukee was. Elayna and I drove back to Missouri, trying to get our arms around what had just happened, then caught a flight to Milwaukee just in time to play on Thursday morning.

I almost didn't have time to catch my breath the rest of the 1989 season. I think it really hit me that I was on tour when I got to La Costa for the Tournament of Champions the next January. I was paired with Greg Norman in the first round. That'll certainly make you feel like you're playing in a different league.

Looking back on that time, I really believe that if I had just gone out and played my game—relying on my scrappiness and ability to get the ball in the hole with my short game—I'd have stayed out on tour all these years. I don't think I would have been a big star or anything, but I'd have been able to make a good living. But being in the middle of all those big, strong guys like Greg Norman, guys who could just pound it out there, made me think that I had to go out there and find a newer, better swing.

Man, was that a mistake. I've been in search of a golf swing my whole career now. That started a stretch of ten years where I bounced around between the Nationwide Tour and the PGA Tour, playing just well enough to keep food on my family's table, but not well enough to put some money in the bank. During that entire time, I gave a lot of informal putting and short-game lessons to tour-player buddies of mine during practice rounds. Those work sessions were taking up more and more of the practice time I was supposed to be using to try to get myself back on the big tour. In the fall of 2000, Elayna told me that if I was going to spend my time on the practice green helping guys with their putting instead of coming home and spending time with her and the kids, then I was going to have to start charging for the time. Since I wasn't making many cuts at the time, it was hard to argue with her.

So, when guys would ask me to help them, I'd give them the standard speech I had worked up: "I'm going to get in trouble with my wife if I don't charge you, so you can pay me $100 or not, but I at least have to ask. . . ." All very confident-sounding, I know, but once I started charging for lessons, guys who didn't know me felt comfortable walking up to me and asking for a lesson. My short-game instruction "business" blossomed from there, mostly because guys I helped started to play pretty well. I was known as a good putter and short-game player, so I already had the players' respect. Word-of-mouth took care of the rest.

I really started to get some exposure as a teacher instead of a player in 2001, when I helped Pat Bates. He and I were buddies from the Nationwide Tour, and he was going through a terrible time with his putter. He visited Scotty Cameron's putting studio and learned the facts about how the putter should swing—things I'll tell you about in Chapter 4. Pat came back to the Nationwide Tour and told me he was ready to listen. Scotty had given him the "why" of how the putter works, and I simply gave him the feel to get the job done. Things finally clicked. Pat went out and putted great, won three Nationwide events that year and got his PGA Tour card back. That gave me some publicity, but more importantly, it gave me confidence that the stuff I was telling people was working.

I'm really sensitive to how what I teach can impact a guy's game, because I know firsthand how easy it is to screw a player up. I was that guy, listening to things that hurt my game instead of helping it, and I don't ever want to be the one doing that kind of damage. Golf at the professional level is a fragile mix of mechanics and confidence, and I feel like my job is to carefully improve the mechanics so that the confidence can grow as a result. The stakes aren't quite as high for the average amateur player, but I'm not interested in taking the fun out of the game for somebody who used to putt okay and now can't find the hole with a map.

Over the past few years, I've been fortunate enough to have some of the best players in the world trust me to help them with their putting. I loved seeing Jay Haas have his best season on tour after incorporating some of the things I teach. Peter Jacobsen came out to see me the week after missing the cut at San Diego, when he was paired with Jay for thirty-six holes. We made some changes to his short game and putting stroke, and he has been kind enough to give me credit for helping him win on the PGA Tour as a fifty-year-old in Hartford in 2003, and collect his first major on the Champions Tour at the Senior Open in 2004. Craig Stadler asked me to look at his stroke. We made some dramatic changes to it, and he hasn't stopped winning money on the Champions Tour yet. Darren Clarke went out the day after one of our lessons and led the PGA Championship.

I don't think I'm any smarter than the next guy—that's not why I can stand in front of you and see what you're doing wrong and make you better. Mr. Lanning kept telling me over and over again that there aren't any secrets, and he's absolutely right. The mechanics of a good putting stroke are right there, waiting to be used if you just get out of your own way. My knack seems to be the ability to tell the story of what the basics should look and feel like, and to get people to free themselves up to try them. I've also been able to watch my friend Rob Akins teach golf and to learn from the way he focuses so completely on each player he sees; he doesn't go by what the clock says when he's teaching somebody. Rob, who works with David

Toms on the PGA Tour, knows what he wants to get accomplished in a certain lesson, and the lesson will take as long as necessary to get that done—whether that's fifteen minutes or two hours. That means the next player on the schedule is sometimes waiting for his lesson, but that player knows he'll get the same undivided attention. I try to take the same approach with my teaching.

I've reached the point where I could fill up my appointment book every week with lessons if I wanted to, and that's certainly enticing for a guy like me, who struggled for a lot of years trying to find some stability for his family. I still get a tremendous charge out of playing tournament golf, and that's not something I'm going to give up doing—especially with the Champions Tour on the horizon.

How will it all shake out? I think you should get your lessons in the next few years if you want them. I'm working with Jim Hardy on my swing, and I'm hitting the ball better than I ever have. When it comes time for the Champions Tour in 2012, I'll be ready. Then you'll have to play in a pro-am to get your lesson.

CHAPTER 2
THE BASICS

. . . .

You bought this book because you want to make more putts. I can help you do that, but before we get to work on your putting stroke, we need to make sure your setup fundamentals look good. If you can put yourself in good position before you make your stroke, and keep that good setup position consistent over time, you're going to have a great chance to roll the ball well.

Guys that do roll the ball really well—like Brad Faxon, Tiger Woods or Dave Stockton—get complimented all the time about how smooth their strokes look. And it *is* true that they have a nice flow. But I know from years of work on my own game and hundreds of hours of watching players with all kinds of strokes on the practice green that the "flow" in a beautiful putting stroke starts with seemingly mundane details like grip, stance and alignment.

The players who get those details right—grip, stance and alignment—almost can't help but hit nice putts. The hands are neutral and set up to work with each other, not against each other. The eyes are in great position to see the line accurately. The grip lets the putterhead rotate back and release naturally through impact. In other words, it looks comfortable and easy. It looks confident. You've got a lot of the work that goes into a solid putt done before you even make the stroke.

Let's go over the different elements of a good setup step by step. We'll start with the grip and work our way through stance and alignment. After that, you'll be ready to learn the stroke and make it consistently.

GRIP

You're going to hear me say the word "natural" a lot through the course of this book. That's because "natural" body positions are the ones that your body will migrate back toward if you don't interfere. For example, if you're standing in a relaxed position, your arms will hang at your sides, not stick out at the elbows or extend in front of

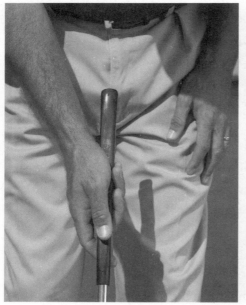

(LEFT) When I put my right hand in place, my thumb runs right down the top of the shaft, and my palm is facing the target. That's a nice, neutral position.
(RIGHT) The grip runs under the muscle at the base of my thumb and along the lifeline in my palm. My fingertips hold the grip in place, not my whole fingers. That's a key component of feel.

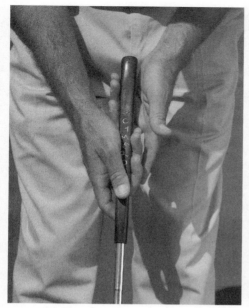 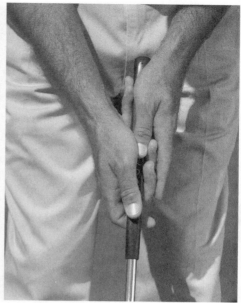

(LEFT) When I'm forming my grip, I put my right hand on first, then open my fingers just enough to slide my left hand into place.
(RIGHT) When my grip is completed, both thumbs run parallel to each other, and my hands are neutral and directly opposite each other.

you. And however your hands hang is how you need to place them on the grip. So obviously, if you can put your hands on the club in a neutral, natural position—one that takes advantage as much as possible of the way your body is naturally put together—you won't have to manipulate them to keep the putter in good position through the stroke.

When it comes to the grip, I want your hands to be on the putter in a natural position relative to the way your arms hang in front of your body. That means they should be positioned parallel to each other, and the back of the left hand and palm of the right hand (for right-handers) should be square to the target at address. Most people hold the putter in a way that gets their hands working against each other, instead of flowing together. In right-handed players, the left hand is usually shifted into a too-weak position (turned toward the target), while the right hand gets too strong (turned away from the target). If the left hand is weak, the face of the putter tends to open on the way through impact, which shoves putts as well as causes pulled puts. The easiest way to make sure your hands are in a neutral position is to check your thumbs. They should run straight down the top of the grip, not angle away from each other.

Having the hands in a neutral position is just the first step. The next piece of the puzzle is getting the handle of the putter in the right position in the hands. When you hold a club for a full shot,

By setting my right-hand grip along the lifeline in my palm and not in my fingers, the putter shaft runs in a line with my forearm.

you've got the handle in your fingers, and an imaginary line from the butt of the club would extend below your arms, toward the middle of your stomach. From this position, it's easy to make the wrist hinge you need in a full swing. You don't use a wrist hinge in a putting stroke, so when you putt, you need to have the handle of the putter running much more in the palms, along the lifeline. This lines up the shaft of the putter with your forearms—the position it needs to be in for the putter to swing on the correct plane.

When I let the grip drift into my fingers, notice how the shaft hangs below the line of my forearm.

I use a reverse overlap grip on my putts—my left index finger extends outside my right hand, and runs straight down the shaft, on top of the knuckles of my right hand. (As a comparison, in the regular overlapping grip you'd use for a full shot, the little finger on the right hand sits between the knuckles of the index and middle fingers.) With the club in my lifelines and the reverse overlap grip, I feel like I have a lot of open space in some places between my hands and the grip. You can even see the light coming through between my hands and the grip in some of the pictures we took for this book. The overriding idea is that the hands and arms should feel soft and responsive, not tight and restricted.

If you're used to holding the putter really tightly in the fingers, this kind of grip is going to be a big change for you. The pressure points are dramatically different—down in the fingertips instead of closer to the palms. In the beginning, it might feel like you've got less control of the putter with my grip, but the opposite is actually true. Your fingertips are the most sensitive part of your body, and it can only help your feel and control to have them more involved in your putting. I've had people tell me that when they work on the grip I teach, it tends to relax their arms and shoulders after a few minutes because they aren't holding the putter so tightly in their hands. A key part of what I teach is getting people in position to get out of the way of their own talent. This grip encourages you to use the touch and feel you already have. Can anybody do it? Absolutely. If you can sign your name, you can develop touch and distance control in your putting. Just think about where you hold a pen when you write something. It isn't in your palm.

This kind of grip gets the top of your forearms aligned along your target line. It's a lot like pointing a gun. If your left forearm gets higher than your right at address, you're going to lose the putt right if you don't make some other compensating move, like closing the face of the putter at address or flipping the face closed with your hands through impact. The opposite is true, too. Get that right forearm higher than the left and you'll have a tendency to pull putts left.

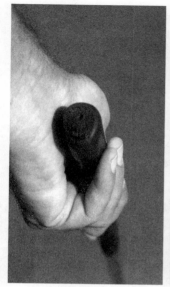

(LEFT) See the space between my hand and the grip of the putter? I'm not wrapping my fingers around the grip. The pressure points are my lifelines and my fingertips.

(CENTER) From this angle, you can see the reverse overlap—my left index finger is running along the outside of the knuckles of my right hand. In a regular overlapping grip, for a full shot, my right little finger would be overlapping.

(RIGHT) The first two fingers of my right hand have the most feel—if I was going to pick something small up from the ground, I'd use them. In my grip, those fingers control my feel.

You'll have to use your hands to compensate for that move, too, by holding the face open through impact. As you might have guessed, that isn't the most consistent way to putt. When those forearms get misaligned, it's really hard to take the putter back on the right path and get the ball to go where you want it to. If I can get you to follow only one piece of advice when it comes to your grip, it'd be to set your hands so that the forearms are aligned. That can offset a lot of other errors.

STANCE AND ALIGNMENT

Once you've got a good grip on the handle of the putter, you need to set up the ball in a good position and aim yourself at your target as precisely as possible. Getting back to the "natural" theme I talked about in the grip section, my stance advice falls along the same line. If you and I were having a conversation on the practice green, you wouldn't stand there with your feet spread far apart, or so close together that they were almost touching. The same should be true for your putting stance. Your feet should be shoulder width apart or even a little bit closer together, so that you're in a comfortable, balanced position. A relatively narrow stance also helps the shoulders turn slightly with the stroke, not rock up and down as they would from a wide stance.

(LEFT) The tops of my forearms are aligned with each other and square to the target line. Get this alignment wrong—one forearm higher than the other—and you'll struggle to consistently hit it where you aim it.
(RIGHT) You can see the change in alignment here. My right forearm is set up higher than my left, which will cause me to miss putts to the left.

I also like you to be tilted forward toward the ball from the hips, not slumped forward with a curved spine or standing too upright. Tilting from the hips will let you swing the putter very easily on a good path and release it with no extra effort. From a slumped position, your elbows actually get too far behind your body, and you're forced to manipulate your hands to hit a putt. A too-upright setup isn't as common, but when it happens, you're forced to rock the shoulders up and down instead of turning them. It's also an awkward, nonathletic position that doesn't let you take advantage of your natural reflexes and senses.

From a nice, tilted position, you want your eye alignment slightly inside the ball. Contrary to what you've probably heard, research shows that the vast majority of good putters have their eye line inside the ball, not over it. Scotty Cameron shared with me that for

(LEFT) To determine where your eye line sits in relation to the target line, get into your posture and hold a ball next to your left eye. Drop it and watch where it lands.
(RIGHT) The ball should land just inside the target line and an inch or two to the right of the ball you'd actually hit with your stroke.

right-handers, the left eye needs to be one inch inside and one inch to the right of the ball. The way you check that is to get into your posture and hold a ball next to your left eye. Let it go and it should land inside the target line an inch and just to the right of the ball on the ground. I believe this is a simple fundamental that matches the fact that golf is played to the side of the ball, swinging on a tilted plane.

A good grip is going to put you in good position when it comes to your arms and shoulders, but it's important to keep these other setup fundamentals in mind. Your arms should feel very relaxed and sit close to your sides at address. I have a very conscious feeling of my elbows being "soft" at address and resting right up against my rib cage. If you feel like you have to reach or extend your arms to

(LEFT) In my putting setup, my feet are as far apart as they would be if you and I were standing here talking. My elbows are soft and close to my sides, and the shaft of my putter is leaning slightly toward the target.

(CENTER) In this good setup postion, I'm tilted at the waist, but my spine is pretty straight and my chin is up from my chest.

(RIGHT) If you let your weight get over your toes, your tendency will be to slump your spine and let it curve down toward the ball. Aside from being uncomfortable, this position prevents you from making a free-flowing putting stroke.

(LEFT) Here, my elbows are sticking out, away from my sides, instead of resting in a relaxed position next to my sides.

(CENTER) Here, my hands are set too low, which forces the putter to go back too far to the outside.

(RIGHT) My hands are set too high, It's hard to make a natural stroke from this position because the wrists have to get too involved to compensate.

get the putter to the ball, you're not standing close enough to it. You also want your shoulders almost level with the ground, with your left only slightly higher than your right (for a right-hander). A common mistake is to get the right shoulder too low in the setup, which promotes a shoulder rock instead of a turn during the stroke. Again, you're trying to set up so that you're very neutral at address, so that you won't have to make any compensations. Your weight should be evenly spread across your feet from left to right and heel to toe. You should feel like you can stand in your putting stance as long as necessary without losing your balance or shifting from foot to foot.

One thing you will notice about moving to a neutral setup is that it will be much easier to maintain consistently. If your old putting setup had some unconventional pieces to it, like a big shoulder tilt at address or an exaggeratedly strong grip, you would have had to make subtle adjustments to your stroke every time you played just to get all the moving parts working in the right sequence.

The next thing we need to talk about is the shaft angle of your putter at address. By pressing the shaft forward (toward the target) or pulling it back (away from the target) at address, you're changing the shaft angle. Many bad putters struggle because they have the shaft leaning backward, away from the target, at address, which pretty much guarantees that they'll start the wrong end of the putter, the grip, back at the start of the stroke. It also pretty much guarantees inconsistent contact. At minimum, I like to have the shaft angle at ninety degrees (straight up and down, when looking from a face-on angle) at address. It's even okay to set up with the shaft pressed a little bit forward, toward the target, which is how I putt. Either way, it encourages you to swing the putterhead away first on the backswing, which is what we're looking for.

After paying all this attention to your grip and setup, don't get careless with your ball position at the end. I like the putterface to be at the middle of the stance, with the ball obviously just ahead of center. If the ball position gets too far forward, you'll run the risk of shifting the shaft angle backward to get the putter behind the ball at address. Move it too far back and the putterhead doesn't have time to fully release, and you'll start pushing putts to the right. Again, a neutral position—with the hands, ball and putter in the middle of the stance—is going to make it easier for you to make a stroke without any compensating moves.

Of course, you can have the greatest grip and setup in the world, but if you don't have good alignment, you won't be able to translate the setup—and your read—into a stroke that sends the ball in the direction you want it to go. I highly prefer a square alignment, so that the forearms, feet, knees, hips and shoulders are all parallel to the line you're trying to putt on. The quickest way to check these alignments is to hold a club across each one. If these lines get crossed—say your feet are open to the target line, but your hips and shoulders are square—you're going to create inconsistencies in your stroke. To hit a putt on line from that position, you're going to have to push your stroke out to the right. That's adding a lot more guessing to putting than I think is necessary.

At least once before every tournament I play, I find a place on the practice green that gives me a ten-footer with no break. I make sure my alignment is good, and I hit straight putts to that practice hole. It's a way of recalibrating my eye, to make sure that when I've got putts with break out on the course, my feet, knees, hips and shoulders are all on the same line. You need to check yourself at least as regularly, because alignment—and ball position—can get out of whack very easily. It's one of the most common things I adjust with the tour players I see—and it's something that happens to them without them really noticing. It's frustrating, because your stroke can feel really great, but the putts just aren't dropping—because you aren't aimed correctly.

ALTERNATIVE STYLES

If you happen to putt cross-handed, or with a long putter or a belly putter, does this mean what I teach doesn't apply? Absolutely not. I'm a fan of more conventional putting styles, but if you do happen to use one of these other methods, you can still benefit from the mechanics in this book. Let me just give you an overview of some of the alternative styles out there, so that if you *do* use one of them, you're getting the most out of it.

Cross-handed putting is probably the most common variation I see, both with tour players and average amateurs. Players usually go to it because they have a breakdown in the right wrist on a conventional stroke. The cross-handed style puts the left wrist in charge of the stroke and locks down that right wrist. If you do putt with your left hand low, you have to be careful about maintaining the line across the top of your forearm that we talked about earlier in this chapter. The cross-handed grip can cause you to get the right forearm lower than the left at address, which affects your stroke. One positive is that a cross-handed grip helps keep a player from getting too much shoulder tilt away from the ball at address.

When I worked with Craig Stadler on his putting, he incorpo-

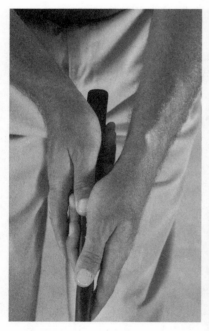

(ABOVE) The principles I teach are the same even when the hands are reversed on the putter. I'm still maintaining the grip up the lifelines, and the hands are neutral.
(RIGHT) My setup with a cross-handed grip is basically identical to what I would do with a standard grip. The cross-handed grip keeps your left wrist flat to the target through the stroke.

rated the stroke I teach, but with one exception—he uses the claw grip. I don't really have a problem with that, because the claw grip helps him swing the putter on the right arc. By placing the right hand parallel to the target line on the grip, instead of with the palm square to the target, you're locking the right wrist in a consistent position, and taking excess hand action out of the stroke. In Craig's case, the claw really frees him up to move the putter in a nice arc around his body. Like the cross-handed technique, the claw also keeps you from getting too much shoulder tilt at address, which lets you swing around your spine instead of rocking the shoulders.

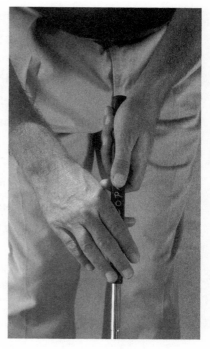

The left-hand grip is the same as the conventional grip I teach, but the right-hand grip is pivoted so that the hand runs parallel to the target line. The biggest benefit of the claw is that it completely removes the hinge in your right wrist.

Longer-length putters are also becoming more common these days. You can use them to make the stroke I teach, as long as you follow a few fundamentals when you set up. With the long putter, you still need to pay close attention to your alignment at address, with the feet, knees, hips and shoulders all square to the target line. The arc of your stroke, which I will go into detail about later, may be less since the shaft angle is very upright because the putter is anchored in the chest. Just make sure that you don't move anything in your body above where the putter is anchored in your chest. Just swing the putter with your right arm, allowing your elbow to hinge, and make the stroke. Take advantage of the consistency of the anchored putter by staying quiet with your shoulders.

The belly putter comes closer to a conventional stroke, with some of the same advantages of a long putter. I like it because it's really hard not to swing on an arc with it. It's got an anchor, but you can still swing both arms like you would with a normal-length putter. The only difference between it and a conventional putter is that it's harder to feel the natural hit and release that comes pretty easily in a stroke with a conventional-length putter. To get the putter to release the way I teach, the left wrist and arm have to break down and bend toward the target. That's not something you'd teach in a conventional stroke, but with the belly putter, it's not wrong. Just look at how Stewart Cink has adapted. You have to do it because the club is anchored. Just keep in mind that the USGA is thinking about banning belly putters because of the way they're anchored to the body during the stroke. If that happens, you'll be forced to go back to something more conventional, so you might not want to get too attached to it.

CHAPTER 3
FINDING THE
RIGHT EQUIPMENT

. . . .

Your putting stroke obviously has to be sound if you want to roll the ball consistently. Learning the basics of grip, stance and setup will help you make a consistent stroke, but if you want to take advantage of that stroke, you have to have equipment that's going to let it happen.

I agree with the general idea that a player should use a putter that feels good and sets up in a way that's attractive to the eye. But all putters are not created equal. If you believe that the putter should swing on an arc, like I do, that means you should pick a putter that has certain physical characteristics that make it easy for that to happen. In general, a putter that is more heel-shafted versus center-shafted, and weighted with toe hang versus face balanced, will give you a more effective putter for the job. It's important to understand that face-balanced putters are best suited for players who choose the straight-back-and-straight-through method. You're going to have a hard time getting the stroke I teach to work for you if you're doing it with a face-balanced putter. To determine how your putter is weighted, balance it across your index finger. The face-balanced putter's face will point squarely at the sky. If the toe hangs below the heel, you have what we're after.

I use a modified Scotty Cameron Newport model now, and

I like my putters to have "toe hang," which means weight is moved toward the toe of the putter, to promote a swing that moves on an arc. On a face-balanced putter, the face of the putter points straight up in the air when I balance it on my finger.

I've always used a putter with that style head, ever since Mr. Lanning gave me my first Ping Anser putter in 1982.

A putter has four measurements that are really important to get right if you want to putt well: shaft length, weight, lie angle and loft. A player can certainly adapt his or her stroke to the putter by making a setup change, or by changing the way he or she hits the ball, but to me, adding compensations like that means adding the potential for inconsistency.

The whole idea behind the way I teach people to set up for a putt is to get the body in a neutral position. What I mean by neutral is simply having your body lined up squarely, your weight distributed evenly on your feet, your hands on the club square, your arms relaxed to your sides and your upper body tilted properly from the hips. I know what is simple often has many aspects, but the key is to find a comfortable, neutral setup position and fit the putter to you, not fit your stroke to a putter that isn't right for you.

If you play with a putter that is too short, or has a lie angle that's too flat or too upright, you're probably going to have to change out of one of the nice, neutral setup positions we've been working on. That doesn't mean you won't be able to make a putt—the human brain is pretty smart, and it'll do its darnedest to subconsciously get the ball back on line—but you're going to have a whole lot more trouble aiming consistently from a non-neutral position.

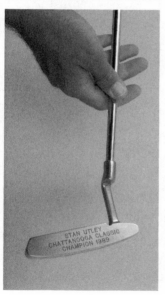

(ABOVE LEFT) Mr. Lanning gave me my first Ping Anser putter—just like this one that came out of his bag—when I was twenty. This was the putter he used to teach me the method I share with people now. It's thirty-six inches long and has the flat lie angle and loft that I like.

(ABOVE CENTER) My dad gave me this Jerry Barber model putter when I was fourteen. The thing I remember most about it was that it had a sticker on the shaft that said WORLD'S GREATEST PUTTER. I thought that was supposed to be me.

(ABOVE RIGHT) This is the Anser putter I used to set the PGA Tour record—six putts in nine holes (more on that in a later chapter). It's built to fit me, and it's almost identical to Mr. Lanning's putter. The putters I've used since 1982 have all looked pretty much the same.

(LEFT) Any player who wins a PGA Tour event with a Ping putter receives a gold replica of the model from the company. It's an amazing feeling when you open the box and see it for the first time. It's an exclusive group of people that gets one of these. I've hit a putt with it, but it's a little light to actually use.

Let's start with shaft length. When you get fitted for irons, the clubfitter wants to give you clubs that allow you to comfortably reach the ball from a good setup position. The same holds true for the putter. Once you are set up in the neutral position we just talked about—a setup that establishes your most comfortable tilt over the ball—I want the putter to be just long enough so that your arms hang with a slight bend in your elbows. Remember, the feel you're looking for is soft arms close to the sides. From this position, you've got to have a putter that's long enough to reach the ground. For most people, that means at least thirty-four to thirty-six inches. Again, using something shorter will force you to make other compensations and get away from a neutral setup. If your putter is too short and you have to extend your arms into a straight or locked position, it will encourage you to move your body excessively in the stroke. Essentially, a short putter sets you up too close to the ball, which translates into a more upright shaft angle. The heel of the putter will tend to lift off the ground, which causes the putter to aim right. You'll need to compensate for that.

If the putter is too long—which I rarely see—your posture will likely be too tall, or your elbows will be bent too much and you'll lose the feel of the proper arm swing. You'll be too far from the ball, which lifts the toe of the putter off the ground. The short putter moves your aim to the right, while the too-long putter does the opposite, with the lifted toe pushing your aim to the left.

Once you've established a good putter length for yourself, swingweight is another important element to consider. This is very personal. My preference is a putter that has a swingweight similar to my irons, which is D-2. It is very common today for players to prefer slightly heavier putters that swing at D-6 or D-8, and most standard putters come in this weight. This is something you'll have to experiment with yourself. Just keep in mind that swingweight is going to have a significant impact on your tempo and feel. A heavier putter wants to move in a longer, slower stroke, while a lighter putter is better for a faster, more aggressive stroke. My advice about your stroke doesn't change based on how heavy your putter is, but the weight of the putter you pick should match your tempo and stroke characteristics.

Lie angle works in a similar way to shaft length. From the neutral position we've been talking about, you need to have a putter that not only reaches the ground, but sits flat on the ground at address. If your putter has a lie angle that's too upright, the toe of the putter will be coming off the ground at address, and you'll have a tendency to aim to the left of your target. If the lie angle is too flat, the toe of the putter will be on the ground, but the heel will be up in the air. Having the correct lie angle will give you the best chance to aim properly and make solid contact time after time.

The least understood putterhead measurement is loft. Everybody knows how loft works on a driver or an iron: If you buy a driver with 9.5 degrees of loft to replace a driver with 8.5 degrees of loft, and everything else is equal, you're going to hit your tee shots higher in the air. A 4-iron has less loft than a 6-iron, and so on. Even your putter has loft on it—usually three to four degrees when it comes from the factory. Putters have loft because the ball sits down slightly in the turf, not like it would on a hard surface like a tabletop. You need some loft to be able to get the ball out of that depression and rolling on its way. If you don't have enough loft on your putter at impact, you'll be hitting the ball into the side of its depression, and it'll lose speed and bounce offline. If you have too much loft, you'll send the ball up into the air, almost like a little chip, with backspin. This is certainly not how you want to roll your putts.

Now, you might not have been aware of the role that loft plays in your putter, but I bet you've made subconscious adjustments to your stroke because of it, especially if you're a pretty good putter. I firmly believe most players don't have enough loft on their putters, and it causes some serious problems in the stroke. Once again, the better players can sense when there isn't enough loft on the putter. It's really a subconscious thing. The natural reaction is exactly what you'd expect: When you get to the ball in your putting stroke, you flip the wrists slightly to try to hit up on the ball and get it rolling. It is very, very hard to putt consistently that way. By simply switching to a putter with more loft—mine has a little over five degrees of loft, instead of three—you take away that subconscious need to hit up on the putt to get it rolling, and your impact becomes much more pure. I've been using a putter with at least five degrees of loft for almost twenty years, and I've never had a problem with the ball shooting up in the air when I hit it. You won't, either.

How does this relate to the average putter you buy off the rack from a golf shop? A standard putter usually has a lie angle of seventy-one degrees, and about three degrees of loft. After I've spent some time with a player and have had a chance to bend their putter with my lie-loft machine, most people fall somewhere around sixty-nine degrees of lie angle and five degrees of loft. I've got sixty-eight degrees of lie angle and five-and-a-quarter degrees of loft on my putter, which works well with the forward press I use at the start of my stroke.

The goal in all of this is to produce enough loft at impact so that the ball rolls true. That can't happen if the shaft is leaning backward, away from the target, when you hit the putt. Even an experienced putter might get the shaft leaning that way because his putter doesn't have enough loft—and he might not even know why he's doing it. I see this happen all the time with tour players. I don't think a professional would intentionally putt with the shaft leaning backward, but if that's what it took to get the ball rolling, he would do it to try to get the ball rolling true.

Ever since I started out on tour, players of all skill levels—from beginner pro-am partners to elite tour players—have always thought my putter looked and felt good. It's because of the flatter lie angle and extra loft I've always used. It just makes you feel like you don't have to work as hard to get the ball to roll nicely. But keep in mind that loft should be combined with a flatter lie angle. That's what makes my putter feel so good. Just jacking up the loft on your putter without addressing the lie angle will give you problems. Add loft to a putter with an upright lie and the face will look hooked.

The point of all this is to reinforce the idea that it's important to get a putter that fits you—just like you'd get irons or a driver that fit. It's very, very common for me to watch a player at the start of a putting lesson and see that he or she is doing some things in the stroke to compensate for the putter. I have one of Scotty Cameron's portable lie-loft machines (it even fits in the back of the cart), and I can measure and bend the putter right there on the practice green. It's amazing how much better your stroke can get just from that kind of adjustment. Again, you're not working against your body, but with it. For me, it's so much fun to work with a guy who shows up with a putter he's not really that in love with, and after two minutes of me bending it up, he's loving it. That's a place we can go to work from.

(LEFT) I have one of Scotty Cameron's lie-loft machines, which lets me bend putters to precise specifications in just a minute or two.
(RIGHT) The simple gauge tells me what lie angle the putter has. This one has seventy degrees—one degree flatter than what a standard putter comes with. I like putters to have between sixty-eight and seventy, because it encourages the putter to move on an arc.

When it comes to the putter grip, I'm interested in getting maximum feel for what the putterhead is doing, which means I want a grip that is relatively thin. I think people who have a lot of feel in their fingers will want that kind of narrow grip. But a guy with big hands or long fingers is not going to want to use a small grip. It has to be comfortable, as though the hands just want to go on there naturally. The one key to a putter grip is to avoid getting one that's too big. I think if you go too big, it takes feel away. I've seen people go with a big grip because they think it takes the hands out of the stroke. That's the wrong way to go about it. You fix a handsy putting stroke by improving fundamentals and understanding what the putter is supposed to do during the stroke, not by sticking a big grip on there. Your fingers are the most sensitive part of your body. I'm not in favor of anything that takes them out of the equation.

There are a lot of putters on the market today. You can spend $30 or $40 at the bargain rack in your local shop and find something you love. A Scotty Cameron Newport like mine can run as much as $300. Technology has certainly played a role in the design of new makes and models. Enlarging the sweet spot, moving the center of gravity in the putterhead and even adding grooves to the face to change the roll of the ball are all good advancements. You can miss the center of the face on some of the new oversize putters by two inches and still get a reasonable roll. If you did that on the putters I grew up on, the ball might go as much as a foot off line on a fifteen-foot putt. That's like missing a free throw by throwing the basketball into the stands. In the end, it's still the person holding onto the club who is responsible for how the ball rolls. When choosing your next putter, or to decide if you've already got the *one*, use your own instincts on how it looks and feels, get the lie and loft adjusted to fit your stroke and use it a long time.

One extra thing I've noticed over the years, both from maintaining my own putters and experimenting with other ones, is that the *appearance* of the face angle on a putter is way, way more important than the *actual* face angle. If you set yourself up in a nice, neutral stance and your putter looks closed—that is, the face appears to be aimed to the left of the target—you're bound to do some bad things with your stroke. I've seen some interesting testing done with lasers attached to the faces of putters, and they show what I had figured to be true just based on my experience. If you *think* your putter is open or closed—or if it really *is* open or closed—at address, you *will* compensate for that with your stroke, because you'll subconsciously believe that the ball isn't going to go in the right direction the way you've got it set up. I like my equipment to be neutral so I don't have to deal with those compensations.

I've had a remarkably consistent career when it comes to the actual putters I've used in competition. I have changed putters only about four times in the last twenty years—mostly due to lost luggage. The Cameron model I use now has a head shape similar to the Ping Anser that Mr. Lanning gave me back before I turned pro, and the swingweight of all of them since 1980 has been the same, to maintain a consistent feel. When I've experimented with different head shapes, I haven't felt comfortable. The results have been good, so why mess with it?

The wild card in all this discussion is "feel." What does "feel" mean? That's one of those things that's really hard to describe, but you know it when you "feel" it. To me, sound has a lot to do with feel. The sound of a solid putt is very distinctive, and I am listening for that sound every time I hit a putt. To me, that's where my idea of feel starts—from the sound the ball makes when I hit it with my putter. That's why I don't use putters with soft inserts in the face. I really want the audio feedback. In fact, I have Scotty Cameron cut a channel in the sole and hollow out some of the material behind the face of the Newport putters he makes for me so that I can really hear the impact. In terms of engineering, it doesn't change the performance of the putter in any way, but I like it because I can tell right away if I didn't hit a putt on the sweet spot of the putter, and that's important information to know. Listen for "solid." It will help you understand

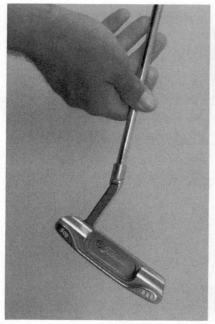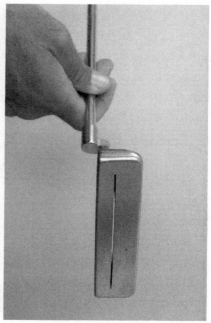

(LEFT) The Scotty Cameron putter I use now has material hollowed out from behind the face to give me more sound at impact. It also makes my putter lighter—a swingweight of D-2 instead of D-6, which is also closer to what my irons swing at.
(RIGHT) My putters also have a groove carved in the sole to add to that sound at impact. I know what a solid hit sounds like, and I want to be able to hear when I don't achieve it.

feel. If you do decide to pick a putter with an insert, pick one that not only allows you to feel solid impact but hear solid impact.

In the end, the mixture of mechanical specs, the way a putter looks and the feel you have for the club itself is something of an art. I've seen guys putt great with beat-up old things you'd be embarrassed to put in a garage sale. I've also seen guys who have great strokes and could get the ball rolling well with a crowbar. What I would say is that a putter with the characteristics I have described here is the most likely to feel good for you, both right now, for the first few putts you take on the practice green, and down the line next summer. You'll be far less likely to turn it into an expensive decoration in the corner of your spare bedroom or closet.

CHAPTER 4
THE ART OF PUTTING

· ·

Wh+at is a putting stroke, anyway?

Sure, the idea is to get the ball in the hole. You can do that a lot of different ways. To use some current examples, take Brad Faxon and Billy Mayfair. Brad has a gorgeous putting stroke. I could watch him hit putts all day. Billy's stroke is different, with the heel of the putter up in the air and an outside-to-outside loop. I'm not criticizing it, because Billy has won a lot of money with that stroke. But I know how hard Billy has to work to keep his stroke sharp. Brad Faxon can get out of bed and stroke the ball great. Like I said, you can stroke the ball a lot of different ways, but I believe that it's easier to consistently be good when you have a fundamentally sound stroke.

There are two schools of thought when it comes to the fundamentals of the putting stroke. One way to putt is to try to keep the face of the putter square to the target line through the entire stroke. Face-balanced putters are designed to work with this type of stroke, and Dave Pelz has done very well teaching that style. Loren Roberts has made miles of putts using that technique, too. But I believe the square-to-the-target-line method works counter to what your body wants to do, and counter to what you do with the rest of your clubs on full shots. It also takes a lot of practice to maintain. That's fine for tour players, who spend hours every week on the practice green, but a challenge for the recreational player.

In my opinion, the putting stroke shouldn't be fundamentally different than a full shot, just a smaller version of it. I love to use the phrase "golf is a side-on game," which I learned from instructor Jim Hardy. You stand to the side of the ball when you hit it, and the shafts in your clubs, putter included, don't run straight up and down from the clubheads. Because you're to the side of the ball when you hit it, the swing has to happen in a round or circular motion. The tilt of that circle is dictated mostly by the shaft angle at setup. This swinging in a circle at a tilt is what causes the swing plane you've seen in so many golf instruction diagrams.

Here's a better way to illustrate what I'm saying. If I swung really, really fast with my putter—say ninety miles per hour—but I hit the ball with my method, it would still go straight. If I did that with the straight-back-straight-through method, that ball would slice, and I'll explain why in a second. I believe that the straight-back-straight-through method is based on the premise of swinging on an axis that is fairly vertical. The eyes are over the ball, and the shoulders rock up and down the target line in order to make the swing work. To me, that doesn't make sense when you're standing to the side of the ball with a club that doesn't swing on an axis that is straight up and down.

Without going into too much physics mumbo jumbo, the clubface on a full swing moves in a way that's square to the arc, not square to the target line. Since I believe the putting stroke is simply a smaller version of a full swing, that means the putter should follow the arc back and through, and stay square to the arc the same way. It will swing slightly inside the target line on the way back, and slightly inside on the way through. It will look like the face of the putter is opening and closing, but that's happening because of the natural rotation of your body, the arms and shaft around the swing plane, not by any conscious twisting or flipping of your hands.

But wait. You're probably thinking that swinging the putter inside the target line can't possibly be as precise as bringing it straight back and straight through on the target line, right? If the putter is doing all this "opening" and "closing," that can't be as good as keeping it square to the target line, right?

Actually, I believe that's wrong.

If you're standing to the side of the ball to hit a putt, to make the putter go straight back and straight through along the target line, you have to use the small muscles in your hands to *close* the putter face on the backswing, and then *open* it again on the forward swing, in relation to your body. That's the opposite of what you do for anything else in this game, from a driver swing to a short pitch, and it's also not the best way to do something consistently, time after time, without a lot of practice.

Letting the putterface move in a path square to the *arc* is what will make the ball go where you're aiming, with a bigger margin for error and less need for practice. That's why Brad Faxon can walk onto a practice green, drop a ball and immediately start rolling it great. He's working with physics and the mechanics of his body, not against them. When I give a putting lesson to somebody, the first thing I usually hear is, "Hey, this is the same thing my full-swing teacher is telling me about the rest of my game." It all comes from the same fundamentals. As I said earlier, I don't believe the putting stroke should work any differently than the swing you'd use for your other clubs. It's just smaller.

To get the putter following that nice path, you need to feel the way the shoulders and arms work in the putting stroke. You're trying to get away from rocking the shoulders up and down and toward turning them around your spine, like they do in a full swing. In other words, if you're a right-hander, it should feel like your left shoulder is moving around toward your chin on the backswing, not down toward your left foot.

The stroke itself is simple: You always want to start the putter-head back first, because the toe of the putter has the farthest to swing on the arc. To make your stroke with a relaxed arm swing, you want to feel your left arm push the putterhead away while allowing the right elbow to soften and fold close to your side. The through swing is generated mostly by lengthening your right arm through impact, in order to have your shaft end up even with or slightly leaning ahead at impact. Your left elbow must respond to this by softening and folding along your left side. If your tendency has always been to work the face square to square, you will need to feel your forearms rotate during the stroke so the toe end of your putter leads the heel in the backswing and then releases through on the arc and leads the toe again past impact. Remember when we talked about keeping the arms and shoulders soft and tension-free? This is where that softness comes into play.

Most players have too much tension in the shoulder and elbow joints when they putt—sometimes to the point of total lockdown. Even if you know what you're supposed to do with the putting stroke, it's impossible to actually do it when you've got that kind of tension. In a lot of the lessons I give, the first thing I start with is tapping the player on the shoulders with the grip of my putter to get him or her to "let the air out" and relax. You'll see a person's shoulders drop three or four inches after that.

When you have that kind of tension in your shoulders and arms, the only way to hit the ball is to use a lot of body movement and release the putter in a flip move with the hands. That causes a tremendous amount of inconsistency—basically, you're making a different stroke every time you hit a putt. It's probably not a surprise to hear that inconsistency like that translates into poor speed control and missed putts. You can guess what happens next: The missed putts build anxiety, which creates more tension in the shoulders and arms. It's a vicious cycle. From there, it doesn't take long to get completely locked up over putts, especially those important five-footers. You're standing over them all tense, with no real idea of what you're supposed to do. There's no feel in that stroke, and no flow.

Other players might have that tension in their putting stroke because of their personality. If you're a precise, detail-oriented person, you might think that locking down the muscles in your chest, shoulders and arms gives you more precision and control in the stroke. Actually, the opposite is true. You need the softness to make it happen. Loose, relaxed muscles in the chest, shoulders and arms will let you respond to the weight of the putterhead moving, and you'll quickly notice how naturally this folding and unfolding takes place. This relaxed, flowing stroke is the best way to hit consistent, accurate putts.

If you have trouble visualizing what I mean by soft, responsive arms, think about tossing a ball underhanded toward a target on the floor five feet in front of you. If you stiffened your arm and tried to toss the ball just using your shoulder, you wouldn't get much power on the toss and you certainly wouldn't have much accuracy. I really like the underhanded toss analogy, because it works for the grip as well as for the feeling of softness in the stroke. If you were going to toss that ball, you would hold it in your fingertips, because that's where your feel is. You wouldn't hold it in your open palm, or grab it in a tight, hand-dominated grip like you would something you were trying not to drop. Your putting grip is the same way. With the underhanded toss, your fingertips are helping your brain automatically judge how much energy to put into the job of getting the ball to move, without too much conscious interference from you. If you have a good grip and keep that softness in your arms and shoulders, you're doing the same thing—letting your brain's powerful natural instincts take over.

Once you relax and make the stroke I've been describing, you'll definitely notice that the putterhead looks like it's opening and closing—not staying square to the target line back and through. That's great, because I believe that's the best path for a putter to travel if you're looking for consistency and a feel for distance. Check out the sequence pictures of my putting stroke in the color insert section and see for yourself. Again, that comes from turning around your spine tilt, on plane, and from the blending of forearm rotation in the backswing and follow-through, not from your hands flipping or turning the grip end like a doorknob.

Explaining how the forearms work may give you more of an idea of what I'm talking about. At address the two bones in your forearms are stacked on top of each other. The top bone is the called the humerus, and the bottom one is called the ulna. In the backswing, make sure you've got the top bones in your forearms—the humeruses, for all you orthopedic surgeons out there—leading the way both back and through. If you rock the shoulders instead of turning them, or close the putterface going back, you'll immediately see the bottom bones in the forearms, the ulnas, leading. Again, the stroke is a combination of shoulders turning, arms swinging and forearms rotating—not wrist action—so maintain the angle you had in your right wrist at address and don't let the left wrist break down toward the target through impact. If you haven't picked up a putter and tried the stroke I teach yet, that might sound like a difficult thing to do. Your impulse might be to get the hands and wrists involved in the stroke—especially at impact—to help generate enough power to get the ball to the hole. It doesn't work that way. Trust me. Forearm rotation and a little arm swing will give you all the power you need. In fact, when you try my method, you'll probably smack the first few putts quite a bit past your target. That's okay. It just means that you can now take a smaller, smoother and more controlled stroke on every putt. You'll quickly get the feel and be able to recalibrate your distance.

To get the ball to roll nicely, you need to move the putterhead end of the club the most in your stroke, not the grip end. The energy in your stroke needs to be primarily in the putterhead through impact—for consistency and efficiency. To start the stroke, the shoulders turn slightly, the arms have a little swing to them, the grip end stays relatively quiet, and the putterhead swings away long enough to create the energy to roll the putt the proper distance. Problems start to creep into the stroke when you turn the shoulders too much, or jerk the grip end of the putter back. You're taking away energy from the end of the club that will be doing all the work, and this will destroy your consistency. If you do move the grip end too much and too early, you have to speed up the clubhead end of the putter down through impact to compensate. The only way to generate that speed at that point in the stroke is to do it with your wrists and hands. The left wrist breaks down, the hands flip toward the target and it gets really hard to make a solid, consistent strike on the ball. You've probably felt those kinds of misses in your hands—a thin, clacking kind of impact toward the bottom of the putterface, which often leads to putts ending up short of the cup.

By far the hardest habit to break is that of tilting the shoulders up and down during the stroke instead of letting them turn around the spine slightly, like they're supposed to. It's one of the fundamental differences between making a stroke that's square to the target line (the stroke that teachers like Dave Pelz endorse) and one that's square to the arc, as I prefer. Don't get frustrated if you struggle with that early on in this process, using a mix of your old stroke and the new one we're working on. A physical therapist explained to me that our bodies fall into a physical pattern when we perform a certain movement time after time—like putting the wrong way—and it's hard to break that pattern. My job is to help you do that demolition work—to build a set of positive, solid fundamentals to replace the old habits. Some players I work with can change their pattern in twenty minutes or so. It might take you a day or a week, but it'll certainly happen. We can all create the change given the right information and a little encouragement.

We've covered mechanics and stroke pretty thoroughly, but I think the "art" of putting covers something more than just physical stuff. People ask me all the time, "What do good putters *do*, and what do they *think*?" Sure, the technical aspect of putting is part of being great—I can't think of an all-time great with terrible mechanics, or a stroke that wasn't repeatable. But good putters also have this attitude about what they do. They have confidence that they're good, and that they're going to make the next putt, even if the last one did a 180-degree horseshoe and stayed out. We're going to talk more about that in Chapters 6 and 7. Here, I want to talk about some of the great putters I've seen, both from a mechanical and confidence perspective.

If I were making a list of the best putters of all time, the guys on it would all have good technique, but they certainly wouldn't have identical strokes. Jack Nicklaus was the absolute best—nobody made more putts with big tournaments on the line. Did he look relaxed and in the flow like a Ben Crenshaw or a Brad Faxon? No—he got into that familiar crouch, kept everything still and basically pistoned his right elbow to make the stroke. He had a very repeatable stroke, even if it had some unique things about it. More than anything, Jack had an incredible intensity about his putting. He was tremendously focused, and spent a lot of time analyzing his line. That might not be the best method for some guys, but it fit with the way he played the game. And he made a lot of putts. There's a generation of players from about 1965 to 1980 that would give Jack the nod if it ever came down to picking a guy to make a putt to save your life. He'd put a good stroke on it, and you know the pressure wouldn't get to him.

I heard Jack say recently that he never missed a short putt he needed to win a tournament. It's just a given in a long tournament career like his that he missed some here and there. As good as he was, nobody is perfect. But he really believes that he didn't miss any big ones, and I think that's because he was so strong mentally that he has blocked out those negative memories. It was one more thing that helped him to be completely focused on the putt he had in front of him—not on something that happened yesterday or last week.

Guys like Crenshaw and Faxon are at the other end of the spectrum, both in terms of stroke and intensity level. Both guys are really artists—lots of graceful flow and pure athletic ability in the stroke. They have such good strokes that it looks like the ball can't help but go in, and they also have the confidence to trust their strokes and let it go. I really learned a lot by watching both of those guys—not so much from their technique, but from their approach. Ben Crenshaw has mastered getting out of the way of his athletic ability and trusting his reads. Faxon has so much confidence in his stroke that he almost doesn't have to practice. Watching either of them is like watching a really talented musician play up on stage.

Tiger Woods falls somewhere in the middle—he has what I call a very efficient stroke, with great fundamentals, but with the intensity and focus Jack had. If you look at the guys who are considered good putters on tour now, Tiger is the guy who has the skill, but also backs it up by doing it consistently under pressure. Tiger's mechanics might not look as graceful as Faxon's, but I wouldn't put Brad or myself on the line under pressure instead of Tiger. He stands over big-time Augusta ten-footers with a foot of break as though he's playing a practice round at Isleworth. Of course, it's a bit of a self-fulfilling prophecy—Tiger has lots more chances to hit pressure putts because he hits it and putts it so well in the first place. All of that big-moment experience gives him such an advantage compared to a lot of guys on tour. They're standing over five-footers thinking about what it would be like to win a major for the first time. He's standing over the same putt thinking about nothing but making it. And if he doesn't make that one, he's completely convinced he'll make the next one. That's a rare, rare skill.

It's impossible to overestimate how important attitude is to putting. I know for a fact that I miss putts even when I'm making a great stroke if my attitude is bad. If I stand over the ball resigned to the fact that I'm probably not going to make it, I won't unless it happens by accident. It's incredible how much of an impact your mindset can have. Even when I have a day where it's hard to see the line, or I just don't feel right, I can stand over the putt and trust my stroke. My goal here is to give you the foundation of putting-stroke repeatability. That's really the secret to building confidence—feeling like you're doing something on purpose with your putting stroke. Learning the mechanics and stroke in this book will help you feel like you can do the same thing with your putting stroke—and have a reasonable idea where the ball is going to go—time after time. Once that happens, you'll start to experience something kind of cool. Instead of getting discouraged, you'll be mad about missing putts you should have made. That's part of the attitude I'm talking about. Guys like Brad Faxon really stand over putts thinking they're going to make every one, and are honestly surprised when they miss, even though they totally understand the reality that they won't all go in. You might not quite get to that point—after all, Brad's about as good as you can get with the putter—but it's a great goal to shoot for.

CHAPTER 5
THE PSYCHOLOGY
OF PUTTING

. . . .

Tour players spend hours every week working on the fundamentals we've been talking about over the last few chapters, making sure they're comfortable with the stroke and getting ready to take it out on the course for competition. If you have decided to make some changes to your own stroke, you'll be doing the same thing on the practice green, hitting putts and experimenting with the things I've been talking about, finding out if they will work for you.

But the practice green is different from the first green in a real round of golf—whether you're playing in the B-flight of your club championship or trying to win a professional tournament. The psychology of putting is all about getting your real-world putting stroke to look as close to your pressure-free practice green stroke as possible, and keeping it that way when the stakes are high. It's about understanding that a good stroke is the best you can do, and accepting whatever happens after that as a part of the game.

You're probably thinking to yourself right now, "Wait a second. Isn't putting all about making more putts?" Yes and no. When I'm standing over a ten-footer for birdie, I'm definitely intending to make it. But I also know there are factors I can't control in the process. I could roll the ball perfectly, and a dent in the green could throw it off line. I've hit plenty of putts that have been—believe it or not—blown off line by the wind. If you set up a machine to roll ten identical twenty-foot putts along the ideal line at the ideal speed, one or two of them wouldn't go in, just because of those imperfections.

If the sole measuring stick of your putting stroke is the number of putts you make, you're going to have some very frustrating days. You can hit great putts that just don't go in. You can also stroke the ball poorly on some days and slam them in off the back of the cup or bounce them in off a spike mark. It's dangerous to get too caught up in either kind of day. On the day you're stroking it good but not making them, it's tempting to start monkeying with your stroke to try to make things happen. That's how putting slumps get started. I work with plenty of tour players who are struggling with their putting simply because they just got away, bit by bit, from the solid fundamentals they used to have. And when you're hitting it poorly but making them, it's easy to get overconfident and miss the signals that you should be spending more time on the practice green.

My treatment for the psychological ups and downs players inevitably go through in putting is to relegate the idea of making putts to secondary importance in the sequence of things to worry about in the pre-putt routine. When I look back on my own professional career, I see a common thread among the four professional events I won, and it stands out like a giant, glowing marker. Three of the four times I won a tournament, I had recently had a conversation with Dr. David Cook, my sports psychologist and good friend. I was really focused on *process*, not *outcome*.

One of the main things David has taught me over the years is the idea that you need to immerse yourself in the process of hitting the putt, not the outcome of the putt itself or the consequences of it. That means building a physical and psychological routine that you go through for every putt that starts from the time you finish your read and ends when the ball leaves the putter. If you've done the first part right, you're really just a spectator for the second part. I know my stroke is good, and if I can put myself in position to make that good stroke time after time, I'm going to make my share of putts.

(THIS PAGE AND NEXT): Face-on view. The one thing that stands out in this sequence is how little I swing the handle on the backswing. Notice how it barely moves until just after impact, when it starts to move toward the target, with the putterhead. In the backswing, the putterhead end is doing all the swinging. In frame 5, I've moved the clubhead back that far with mostly hinge in my right elbow and a little forearm rotation. The impact frame, No. 6, is almost identical to my setup position. Notice the forward shaft angle—the grip end is slightly closer to the target than the putterhead. In the next frame, No. 7, the putterhead has finally released past the grip end. My head is still down—I haven't looked up yet—and the tilt in my shoulders is the same as it was at address. My right shoulder hasn't dipped down, and my left shoulder hasn't lifted. Check out the toe of the putter in the last frame, No. 8. See how it's rotated? My putter has also stayed low to the ground.

(THIS PAGE AND NEXT): Down-line view. My setup position is very square—my feet, knees, hips, shoulders and the tops of my forearms are all in line with the target line. I'm tilting from the hips (not from the waist), which gives me a lot of room to swing my arms without restriction in front of my body. If you slouch in your setup, you're going to feel like you don't have any room. From this angle, you can see just how low to the ground my putterhead stays through the entire stroke. Here, you can really see the arc of the stroke when you look at the position of the ball relative to the putterhead. It goes from the middle of the face (No. 1) to the toe (No. 4), then back to the middle at impact (No. 5) and out to the toe again after the ball is gone (No. 7). In frame 4, you can see my left forearm over my right, and then after impact, my right moves higher, following the arc. Throughout the stroke, I'm not moving much above my elbows. My shoulders don't rock up and down, and they barely turn back and through. You can tell by how consistent the creases in my pants are that my legs don't do anything at all.

5

6

7

8

(THIS PAGE AND NEXT): Up-line view. These pictures were taken from the ball line, and since the putt had a little bit of break, it looks like my shoulders and feet are a little bit open. Regardless of that, you can still see in frame 1 how my forearms are in line with each other. You can get away with open shoulders and feet if this forearm line is square to the target line. It's the most important alignment in putting. Compare frames 1 and 7 and you can see how much shoulder turn we're talking about in a fifteen-foot putt. It's slight. The key thing is that the shoulders don't rock up and down. My left shoulder doesn't lift. You'd be able to tell that this was happening if my putter lifted higher off the ground after impact. I like how the relationship between my arms and chest has stayed pretty consistent throughout the stroke. That relationship changes if you jerk the grip end of the putter back away from the target at the beginning of the backswing, and you really lose consistency there. Keep the relationship the same and you'll get that feeling of flow.

5

6

7

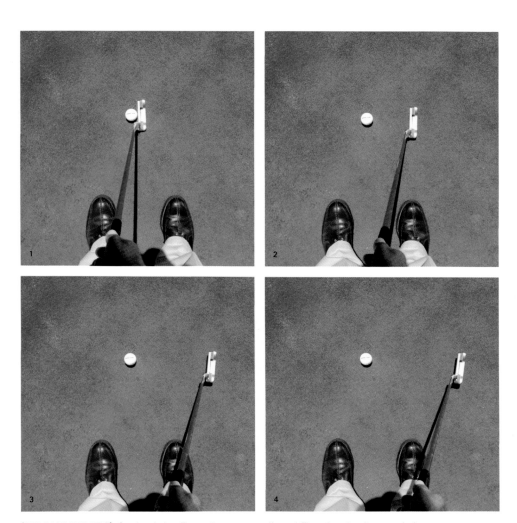

(THIS PAGE AND NEXT): Overhead view. These pictures are really cool. They show just how much the putter moves on an arc for a medium-length putt. Remember, I'm not making an arc with my hands. It's happening with my stroke—a combination of shoulder turn, forearm rotation and elbow hinge. My stroke starts with a slight forward press, which you can see in frame 1. My hands are closer to my front foot than the ball is. Because I'm swinging the clubhead end of the putter, and not shifting the grip, you can see how the shaft angle leans more forward, toward the target, as the putter moves into the backswing. My hands barely get past my right foot. Then, on the downswing, the forward angle gets maintained through impact. Only in frame 6, when the ball is gone, do my hands really start to move forward, moving the grip end of the shaft toward the target along with the putterhead. At that point, my left elbow completely hinges, and my right arm straightens. When you compare frames 5 and 6, you can really see how much the putterhead goes from open to closed. It's moving on the arc, and the putterhead is rotating along that arc. Believe it or not, that's what makes the ball roll true and straight—not sliding the putter up and down the target line while trying to keep it square.

Dr. Cook's technique has two major advantages. First, it helps depressurize the entire putting experience. I don't care if you're playing a $2 Nassau with your friends or trying to make a putt to win a match in the club championship—you're going to be faced with a nerve-wracking putt. It's part of the game, and it's what makes this game great. The more you can immerse yourself in a process-focused pre-shot and putting routine, the more you can distract your mind from the *consequences* of making or missing and concentrate on making a good stroke.

The second advantage is that it helps smooth out the peaks and valleys in your overall putting performance. If you've missed a batch of makeable putts early in a round, it's very, very easy to get discouraged and stand over the rest of your putts that day with some seriously negative thoughts. And trust me, if you don't think you're going to hit a good putt, you're almost always going to be right. Focusing on the process instead of the result liberates you from beating yourself up about something you can't control, and lets you make a much more realistic assessment of your performance.

Sounds great, you say. But how do I do it? It doesn't take anything more than concentration and practice—you don't need any other special skills. It starts with building a checklist to follow before you make every single putting stroke. How dedicated you are to following this checklist will determine how consistent your results will be because of it. Dr. Cook broke the checklist down into five parts for me, and I've found that it works very well. After observing the situation and deciding on your strategy, you then do three things over the stroke—See it, Feel it and Trust it.

First, observe the situation and come up with your strategy. Are you looking at a sixty-footer with ten feet of break? Would a lag up to three or four feet be a great effort? Is it a fifteen-footer straight up the hill that you can be a little more aggressive with? Your green reading (I'll show you how to read putts in the next chapter) and strategy process should happen very early, before you're even thinking about stroke.

See It: Once you've committed to that strategy, get into your putting setup and make your practice stroke. Take the read you've just made and try to visualize the curving line your ball will actually take, and then the ball rolling along that line. It definitely takes a lot of discipline to do it on every single putt, but as it becomes an ingrained part of your process, you'll be able to block out distractions by immersing yourself in the routine. I can tell you from personal experience that when you're coming down the stretch and trying to win a tournament, the adrenaline gets pumping and everything starts to speed up. It's easy to lose control. Having a routine to go through before you putt slows things down and restores your comfort level.

Feel it: Once I finish visualizing the path I want my ball to roll on, I plug in one or two of the swing thoughts I'm playing with on that day. What is a swing thought, and how do I pick one? Good question. It depends. In the process of learning the stroke I teach, you're going to come up with an array of thoughts and feels that help you roll the ball well. Every day I play, I'm applying one or two of those thoughts and feels as the swing key for my stroke. The thought or feel might feel great for two or three days, then start to lose its effectiveness, and then it's time to plug in another one. One day, I might be thinking about rotating the putter with my left forearm to start the putter back. Another time, I'm thinking about moving my left shoulder around toward my chin. I'm physically doing the same thing with my stroke every time. I'm just using a different thought to trigger it. I'm definitely not standing over the ball with a blank mind, stroking the ball toward the hole. I've heard that a few people try to do that—go completely blank—but my mind doesn't work that way. Keeping a single swing thought (or, at the most, two of them) in my head as I make the stroke reinforces my fundamentals and connects the psychological part of putting with the physical mechanics we've been talking about. It's also a great way to keep little mechanical flaws from growing in your stroke. My caddie might notice that I'm picking my putter up a little bit on my backswing. My key for that day might be concentrating on keeping the putter low, and my stroke is better for it.

Trust it: The idea here is not to get overcome with the desire for the ball to go in the hole. We've all been there: Standing over an eight-footer that just has to go in. That desire can easily get in the way of a good stroke in the form of anxiety. By trusting your stroke, you're deciding to give the best effort you can on the mechanics and let the rest just happen. Measure yourself by the mechanics of the stroke, and if you do the mechanical things well, you're going to make some putts. The whole "Trust it" idea also enforces a kind of honesty about your putting game. If you go through the entire routine I've been talking about and, in the end, trust your stroke, you're going to know pretty quickly if you've done enough work on the practice green to develop fundamentally sound mechanics. Poor contact on the toe or heel and bad misses aren't going to make you very happy, but you can use that feedback to get better.

Does all this mean that you're going to be perfectly consistent with the putter? No, we're not machines, and we all go through hot and cold streaks. But having a process helps you understand when and why a streak—hot or cold—is happening, and what to do about it.

The hottest putting streak I had in my career is so vivid in my mind. It's like I was making the putts yesterday. It coincided with the week I won the Louisiana Open Nationwide Tour event in 1995. When I went through that visualization process I just described, the lines looked so obvious, and my stroke was pure. When those two things come together, look out. You'll make them all. It's called catching a case of the drains.

On Sunday that week in Lafayette, I was eight shots behind going into the final round. The wind was blowing so hard that I couldn't even wear a hat. In those conditions, I went out and shot a course-record 62 and made every single putt I looked at—from forty-footers on down. I made ten birdies and had something like twenty-two putts for the day, and ended up beating Keith Fergus by two shots. Ultimately, when you get in the "zone" like that, your own success is what jars you out of it. You start to notice all the putts going in, and even if you try to get out of the way and just let it happen, you start to get tight thinking about trying to make the next one. The streak takes on a life of its own.

The streaks of misses are obviously a little tougher to deal with than when you're draining them all. I've had stretches of a few weeks where I thought I was stroking it well and they just would not go in. I can remember a few times when I needed to hole a four-footer to make the cut, and it just felt like there was no way the ball was going in. Sometimes, it's as simple as going back over your fundamentals and discovering a flaw. For me, it's usually tempo related. Life creeps into my stroke—when life is moving fast, and you've got lots of things to think about, it's easy to get quick with the putter. When I'm going really good, everything slows down and the ball is just squeezing off the putter. For those tougher times, when I can't seem to find the problem in my fundamentals, the way I break that spell is to literally quit trying to make putts. I completely exaggerate the process of disconnecting from the outcome and make a stroke. Let me give you a more specific example.

I was caddying for my friend Lee Janzen at the Players Championship in 2002 and he was going through a tough time getting putts to fall. After a round that left him in the middle of the pack on Thursday, he came to the turn on Friday really needing something to happen to make the cut. I could see how frustrated he was by all the near-misses and lip-outs, and I'm sure he was thinking that none of them were going in the rest of the day. On his ninth green, the eighteenth hole, I took a risk and told him to intentionally aim off to the corner of the hole and try to just miss past the edge of the cup. It seemed to relieve the "I have to make the next one" anxiety he was feeling, and darn it if he didn't hit it right into the heart. He putted great the rest of the day, made the cut and had a good week.

The things that happen to you in streaks just reinforce the overall idea that you should take care of your own business—what you're thinking and how you stroke it—and let the putt take care of itself after you hit it. Go to a PGA Tour event and watch Brad Faxon on the practice green. He won't even go to a hole or set up to any other target. He's out there hitting putts to nothing because he's not trying to make them. He's trying to make sure he's hitting it solid. He knows that if he does, they'll go in. I really like another variation of that kind of practice, something I saw Jeff Brehaut do on the putting green. He sets up to hit a fifteen-footer to no specific target on the practice green, then hits five or six to see where the break actually is. Then he'll use a tee to mark where he hit the putt from, drop a coin where the high point of the putt is, and put a plastic disc down where his first five or six putts ended up. Then he'll practice that putt—to the high point and the coins and down to the plastic disc—making the same smooth stroke. He lets the green determine the break, then practices replicating his mechanics.

CHAPTER 6
ADVANCED TECHNIQUES

· ·

Your stance and setup have improved, and you've got your grip running up the lifelines instead of down in the fingers. Your stroke is looking great, and the ball is rolling nicely. So what happens now? How do you take that from the practice green out to the course?

It starts with the stroke you're making. I really believe that whether you know it or not, you've got enough natural talent that a putting factor like speed control will take care of itself if you can learn to hit your putts solid. Yes, there are other factors—like break, grain and green conditions—that go into making a good stroke, and those are the things we'll be talking about in this chapter. But the first thing you have to remember is that making a good stroke and hitting a solid putt are the most important things you can do. Do that and it's funny how many times the ball seems to run into the hole for you.

Let's talk about reading greens. Ideally, you want to use that great putting stroke you've been working on to send the ball in the right direction. Jack Nicklaus picks a spot in front of his ball and aims for that spot, on both his full shots and putts. I use more of a path technique—I pick out two or three or four objects that my ball may roll over along the way. The most important part is to be able to see the break, and see the line you want the ball to start on. I'm teaching people a stroke that they can hopefully repeat no matter what kind of putt they have. So the goal is to figure out what the ball is going to do after it leaves the putter, so that we can make the ball leave on the right line to curve into the hole. I call it the high point of the break. You're trying to hit your putts so that they start on a line that will get the ball to roll solidly to the high point of the break. The ground takes care of the rest of it.

As a tour player, my green-reading preparation starts days—and sometimes years—before the actual tournament round I'll be playing in. I have a yardage book for every tournament I play in, and the book comes with straightforward measurements like the distances from certain landmarks to the center of the green, and topographical information about each green.

For example, I can look at this chart of the fifteenth hole at Fox Den, where I played the Knoxville event on the Nationwide Tour, and tell you exactly what I'm supposed to do. The notation on the bottom says that the ball really runs on this fairway, so driver is too much. There's no reason to risk hitting it through the dogleg into the trees on the left. The "OK" designations short right of the green tell me where I can miss the green and have the best chance of getting up and down—usually the place where there's flat terrain and short grass, or maybe a big bunker without much of a lip.

I spend a lot of my time carefully drawing arrows on the green to show the fall lines—the ridges built into the surface of the green that have the most influence on how putts will break. Here, you can see a long, gentle ridge in the front-right quadrant of the green, a sharper hump in the back-left section and another hump in the back right. The dots show the different places where pins have been set on the hole. For example, if the pin is set front right, I know I can miss a little to the left of the pin and the ball will funnel toward the hole. And to get to that back-left pin, I know I've got to carry it up onto the tier, or else the ball will kick off the ridge and leave me with a tough putt.

The yardage book is the first piece of the greens-reading puzzle.

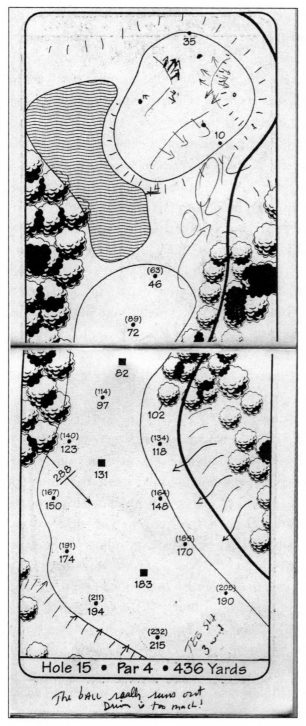

I draw the green contours in the yardage guides I use for each tournament I play in. If I know the general characteristics of the green, it helps me when I'm reading particular putts on that green.

Hole 15 • Par 4 • 436 Yards

Next, I play practice rounds and carefully note what my shots do when they hit each green. Do they feed left or right? Do they tend to check up, or run toward the back of the green? I also pay close attention to the topography of the area around the green as I walk up to it after hitting my approach. Is the area flat, or is there a mountain or valley to one side of the green or the other?

Walking up, I can usually get a general idea of what the green's tendencies are. That way, if I'm torn between two reads later on, I can use that piece of general information about the green to break the tie in my mind. Then I'll hit some practice putts from different spots around the green, taking note not so much of the specific amount of break, but of the general tendencies. What do putts from the front-left corner to the middle tend to do? Are they fast or slow? Does a putt up into the back left break more than I expect, or does it break less than it looks? All of these notes go into the yardage book, which I bring with me year after year. I also draw onto the pages what the tournament-round putts I've faced have done. After three or four years, I've got a pretty good scouting report on just about any pin location they can throw at me.

You might be thinking to yourself, that's fine for a tour player, but how does that help me? If you play at a club, you're in a great position to get detailed information about every green at your course. In fact, if you go out and play without it, it's like leaving a club out of your bag. It's as easy as going out with a little notebook for a couple of practice rounds and recording the general tendencies of the greens. It's amazing what this one step, actually going out and taking notes on your greens, adds to your body of knowledge. You might have a general idea that the green on number four is fast and breaks hard right, but do you really know what a putt from four or five different spots on that green to a front-right pin really does? Go practice them, and you'll never be shocked by what your putt does during a round that really counts.

That kind of information is great to have, but what happens when you're playing a course for the first time? You obviously want to walk toward each green after your approach shot with your head up and your eyes open. You're looking for the overall tilt of the green, which influences the way most putts will break. Once you're actually looking over your putt, there's a straightforward, quick method to deciphering the break. I start by looking at my putt from behind the ball, and then I walk behind the hole and look at it from the opposite direction. When I'm returning to my ball, I make sure to walk to the low side of the hole—the opposite side from where the ball will break—and look at the putt from halfway between the ball and the hole. For example, if I'm looking at a twenty-footer with a foot of break from left to right, I want to look at the break from the right side of the ball, halfway between the ball and the hole. From that position, you get the best perspective on the amount of break the putt will have. This is something I do when I play, and most tour players

Your first read on a putt comes as you're approaching your ball for the first time. You're trying to get an overall sense of the topography of the green.

Next, I move behind the hole, on a line with my ball, and look at the putt from that direction. You often can get a better sense of the break from that side.

On the way back to my ball, I read the putt from halfway between my ball and the hole, on the low side of the break—the opposite side from where the ball will break. This gives me a feel for just how much break to play.

do it out of instinct. I'm emphasizing it very purposefully because Dave Stockton, one of the best putters of all time, told me it's one of the most important things he teaches in his clinics.

Once you look at your putt from that angle, you'll probably wonder if you're really seeing as much break as you think you are. You are. Most amateur players dramatically underestimate the amount of break in the average putt. Add in the fact that many players fixate on the hole and not the high point—where they need to aim the face to account for the amount of break in the putt—and it's easy to see why most putts miss on the low side.

The read itself is one part of the equation, but the type of putt itself is another important thing to consider. When you take into account the topography of the green, keep in mind that a tilt in the green early in the putt is going to have less impact on the roll of your ball than a tilt toward the end, near the hole. In other words, as your ball slows down near the hole, it will take more break than it did when it was coming right off the putterhead. In practical terms, you're doing a general read on the overall tilt of the green for the first ten or fifteen feet of a twenty-footer, then a more detailed, specific read for the last five feet. The same principles hold true when you have a downhill putt. You have to make a smaller, slower stroke to account for the downhill slope, and when your ball is rolling more slowly, it will tend to take even the most subtle break. You can read less break into an uphill putt, because you're making an aggressive stroke to account for the slope. That's why players at every level, from the PGA Tour to the B-flight at the club championship, hate sidehill-downhill putts. They have a lot of side-to-side break, and they have to be hit gently to account for the downhill slope. Get too tentative with them and you leave yourself another downhiller to finish up. Get too bold and you're ten or fifteen feet past the hole.

It's really a golf cliché by now, but you *are* better off leaving yourself below the hole—where you have an uphill putt left—on an approach shot, pitch or chip. You'll be less tentative with your stroke, because you're less worried about knocking it by the hole and leaving yourself a tester coming back. Because the ball comes off the putter faster in the beginning of an uphill putt, it will break less overall, which lets you play the putt straighter. The idea of leaving yourself below the hole is a good one for lag putting as well. On a long putt, say one of fifty or sixty feet, your goal is to leave yourself within five feet of the hole for the next putt. It's obviously better to favor the side of the hole that leaves you something relatively straight and uphill, if possible. That's something I think about automatically when I go through my read and pre-shot routine for a long putt. It's like playing pool. You want to know where your best leave is—the best spot to hit the next shot.

Another small but significant factor in green reading is grain— and that's not just for those of you who play on Bermuda greens. It's been my experience that almost every grass grows in a certain direction. Sure, Bermuda greens have a more pronounced grain that will make your ball move more than closely mown bent grass. But when you're playing on bent and you can see the shine on the greens, that means you're putting with the grain, while a shaded color means you're playing into it. If the greens are already quick, that difference in the direction of the grain is going to make a difference in how hard you have to hit the putt. That's great information to know, and your brain needs to process it at least on a subconscious level.

One other thing to keep in mind when you make your reads is the moisture on the greens. After a night of rain, the greens are obviously going to run a little bit slower. If the sun is out, you can expect those same wet greens to dry out over the course of the day—and dry out even quicker if the wind is blowing. That can make a significant difference in green speed from the time you play the first hole to the time you make the turn. Unless you're in the desert, there's also morning dew to consider. Until that dew burns off, the greens will run slower. If you're in a period of wet weather, the grass at the course will tend to grow more quickly—and the maintenance people won't have as much chance to get out and cut the grass. Longer grass on the green usually translates into slower speeds. The opposite is true as well. In a dry summer (or a standard summer here in Scottsdale, where I live), greens tend to play firm and fast. Those kinds of greens actually make a different kind of sound when your approach shot lands on them—a hollow clunk instead of a wetter thwack.

If you're feeling good about your stroke and you start to make some good reads using the strategies I've been talking about, it's amazing how your speed starts to take care of itself. Your brain can sense factors like uphill and downhill, and when you start reading enough break into your putts, your brain won't be subconsciously trying to yank the putter onto the path that will get the ball started on the right line. That confidence just starts to grow and grow. One of the questions I get over and over again is, "How do I know how hard to hit it?" My answer is that you already know how hard. You just have to put yourself in position to use that information.

So you feel good about the read. Now what? I have a regular physical and mental routine that I follow every time I hit a putt, and it helps me consistently translate my read into where I actually hit the putt. It starts with eye dominance. Everyone has one eye that is dominant over the other, and the dominant eye leads in terms of focusing on a target. You can figure out which of your eyes is dominant by looking up at a target that's pretty far away, like a light or a street sign, and pointing at it without thinking too much about what you're doing. Without moving your finger, try closing your left eye. If your finger is pointing directly at the target, you're right-eye dominant. If your finger is pointing off to the side of the target, you're left-eye dominant.

Why is eye dominance important to know? Because, as you can see from that simple eye test I just described, if you rely on your nondominant eye to line you up with your target, you could be a few inches—or even a foot—off as to where the face of your putter is actually aimed. That means you'll have to do something in your stroke, either consciously or unconsciously, to get the ball back on line. I know I'm right-eye dominant, so I set the putter down with my right hand first, and let my right hand do the aligning of the putter toward my intended line. I've already made my calculations for the

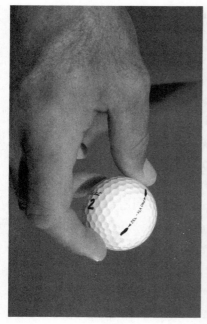

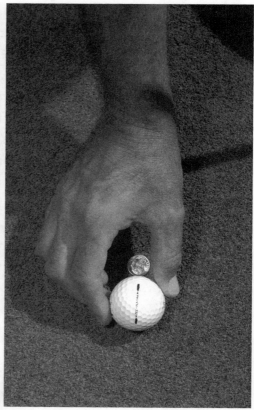

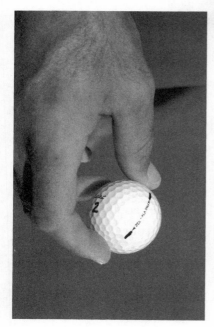

(ABOVE LEFT) I use a marker to make a straight line on my ball, along the model name on the side. Then, when I line up my putt, I place this straight line on the ball directly on the line I want my ball to travel. That way, I have another alignment aid, and I can watch the line on the ball as the putt rolls to see if I made a good stroke. If I can still see the line all the way to the hole, the stroke was pretty pure. If the line disappears, that means I've come across the ball.

(ABOVE) Once I've drawn a line on the ball, I place the ball in front of my marker, aligned with the line I want my putt to start on—not in line with the hole.

(LEFT) I always draw the same number that's printed on my ball right next to the pre-printed figure. I want to be able to identify it easily, even in deep rough.

break and speed, so at this point, just before I pull the trigger, I'm going into the visualization and swing-thought processes I described in the last chapter.

My goal is always to roll the ball as well as I can. Making the putt is nice, obviously, but watching my ball roll nicely is the primary feedback I'm looking for when I hit a putt. A great way to get an instant read on that is to draw a line on the ball. I use a Sharpie-type marker to make a straight line along the model name on the side of the ball. Then, I take a lot of care to align that straight line with the line I want my putt to start on—not on a line with the hole. When I stroke my putt, I want that line to appear as a continuous stripe on the ball as it rolls toward the hole. If the line wobbles, it means I've cut across the ball through impact.

Another question I hear quite a lot from average players I see is about how "aggressive" I am when I putt, or how aggressive the average person should be on regular country-club greens. Again, that depends on what the definition of "aggressive" is. Aggressive can mean that if you're standing on the green with a putter in your hand, you're trying to make the putt—no matter if it's ten feet straight up the hill or forty-five feet down the slope with two breaks. Aggressive can also mean you try to iron out any break in shorter putts by hitting it hard, right at the hole. I'd call my own putting aggressive from thirty feet out to about ten feet out, where I feel like my ability to roll the ball well is going to have positive results. In other words, I'm not trying to simply lag it up there close. From about ten feet and in, I feel like I should make almost every putt. Does that mean I do, or that I feel confident over every one? Absolutely not. When you add in tournament pressure, nerves, fast greens and the funky stroke here and there, you're going to miss a few. But the fact that I feel good about my stroke—and the fact that a good stroke breeds putting confidence—helps put me in a frame of mind where I expect good things to happen when I'm standing over a ten-footer. I feel good about my read and stroke, so I don't usually try to take the break out of a putt by hitting it harder, unless I'm really close, like inside four feet. Unless you're feeling really confident about your own stroke—and you're ready for a three-footer if you miss—I don't recommend that strategy in your own game, either.

What does my level of aggressiveness or confidence in putting mean for you? Well, "success" in putting is a relative term. You want to assess where your own putting is, and turn the dial to more successful results in terms of your own game. For you, that could mean getting a better handle on your long putting and reducing three-putts. It could mean standing over an important fifteen-footer for par and feeling good about your stroke, not absolute dread about what's going to happen next. Maybe you have a very tangible scoring goal—like breaking ninety or eighty for the first time. Some changes to your fundamentals and a small amount of practice—just an hour or two on the practice green each week—can get you there.

You can compare your success to what a tour player can do with a putter, but it's important to keep a few things in mind. First of all, when you watch a tour event on television, it's easy to get the idea that a tour player is a lock to make any six-footer he looks at. Even the putting records themselves are a little deceptive. I set the PGA Tour record for the fewest putts over nine holes at the 2002 Air Canada Championship, with six. Everybody asks me if the hole looked huge that day. Actually, it didn't feel like anything out of the ordinary. I missed a lot of greens and made some nice putts to get up and down, but the big thing was that I chipped in twice. That record is more a testament to my short game than to my putting. Just remember that when you're watching a telecast, you're mostly seeing the six or eight guys playing well and making birdies. Of course they're feeling good with the putter that week. You also have to remember that the average tour player has a tremendous amount of skill and works a ton on his game. Tour players shoot low scores because they hit fairways and greens and make putts, and also because when they miss greens, they get it up and down. If I played in from a ten- or twelve-handicapper's second shot, I wouldn't shoot too many over par.

There's no physical reason you can't take what tour players do in their putting games and use it to improve your own stroke. Just don't beat yourself up when you miss the odd three-footer for par, or three-putt from twenty feet. I take it as absolute truth that the only thing I can control in the putting game is my own stroke. I know that I can make a great stroke and roll the ball great and the putt still might not go in. Maybe my read was a little off, or maybe the green wasn't quite true. What we're trying to do here is improve the average of all your putts—get the bad ones less bad, and the good ones consistently on line. If we can do that, you're going to make more putts, leave yourself less work to do to clean up long putts, and most importantly, enjoy yourself a heck of a lot more out there.

I've given you a lot of technical and procedural information here, but I have to point out one important fact. You can easily get too caught up in the process of reading your putt and disrupt the most powerful tool you have in your putting arsenal—instinct. I can remember playing with Ben Crenshaw in the first two rounds of a tour event many years ago, and I was amazed by the way he seemed to just walk up and hit his long putts without too much of a careful read. My interpretation of that was that he knew that a precise read from thirty or forty feet was impossible, so he was relying on his instincts and a good roll to get the ball close. Of course, when he got closer, he took his time and made a precise read—because he was in a position to take advantage of it.

I'm not suggesting that you walk up and whack your putts with no thought about where they might go. But you want your routine on the putting green to be a mixture of conscious information gathering and positive visualization, and then you want to get out of the way and let your instincts take care of the rest.

CHAPTER 7
FAULTS AND FIXES

. . . .

W hen I'm working with a player—and it doesn't matter if it's a tour player or an average player—what we're doing is exchanging stories. What I'm trying to do is listen to your story—what you're doing with your stroke, or, in some cases, what you *think* you're doing with your stroke. Then I watch you hit some putts.

For the first five or six strokes, I'm looking for your current fundamentals. I want to see how you stroke it, but also how you set up to the ball, what your grip looks like and what kind of stance you have. It's amazing how the puzzle fits together. If I see your stroke going from in to out, nine times out of ten, you're going to have a setup that aims you left. That's because the in-to-out stroke makes the ball go right, and the faults have to offset each other for you to have any chance of sending the ball in the right direction. It isn't some kind of "Rain Man" trick—we're talking about a twenty-inch stroke here, so it usually doesn't take very long to see what's going wrong. Believe it or not, the problems that tour players and average players have are pretty similar. You're dealing with grip and balance issues, or a stroke that is built to accommodate a putter with loft or lie-angle problems. The only difference is the matter of degree.

My ultimate goal is to figure out the best way to tell *my* story, the one you've been hearing for the last six chapters, in a way that you

When I'm working with somebody, I want to watch them hit a few putts first, to get an idea of what they do. It takes only five or six putts to get a feel for a person's fundamentals, and what is necessary for them to change.

can not only understand, but integrate into your own game, too. For some players, it's as simple as showing them the reverse overlap grip I use and how it moves the pressure points down to the fingertips. The grip then releases the tension in their arms, and they immediately get it and start stroking the ball unbelievably well. A really talented tour player can usually "get it" in an hour or two, and feel comfortable in a couple of weeks. It might be a half hour on the putting green, and then a few bends on the lie-loft machine to get some more loft on your putter. That's been enough to get some players off and running right away.

Some players take longer to get comfortable, either because they've got more complicated stroke problems to work out, or because what I'm telling them is far away from where they were. It's at this point where the art of teaching really comes in—something I've learned from great full-swing instructors like Jim Hardy and Rob Akins. You can feed a player only as much as he or she can digest at one time. Usually, that means one or two "thoughts" or "feels" in a lesson. Sometimes, that takes ten minutes to get across, and sometimes that takes two hours. People learn in different ways. Some players want me to show them how I do it, and then they try to copy what I'm doing. Others respond better when they set up to putt and I physically guide them through a stroke with my hands on their putter. Other people respond really well to descriptions and anecdotal examples, and want to be left alone to fool with what I've told them all on their own. Getting through to each kind of player is the challenging part of what I do—not actually giving out putting advice.

If I had you in one of my three-hour clinics, there'd be plenty of time to give you an overview of the putting stroke I teach, and after watching you hit some putts, my objective would be to send you home with enough simple basics to move toward a more efficient stroke. My main interest is getting you feeling better about your game so you can make more putts. Your stroke doesn't have to be perfect to do that, so I'm going to start by picking the few significant issues you've got—the ones that you'll benefit most from correcting—and giving you some tools to address them. Many players—and I'm including tour players in that group—come to see me without any idea of where "better" is from the point they're at. They don't know how to take the next step. Even if I can't solve your problems in an hour, hopefully you'll learn where "better" is in our time together, and you'll be able to practice on your own and recognize it when you make steps in that direction.

The process I go through in a clinic with a half-dozen fifteen-handicappers isn't fundamentally different than the one I use with the tour players who visit me in Scottsdale. As I said earlier, the problems tour players commonly have with their putting are the same problems you have. The degree might be different, but the fundamentals apply to everybody. Before we ever get involved in trying to make putts in a real hole, we work on the setup and the stroke itself, and getting those things nailed down. Once you're feeling good

A grip or an alignment change can make a tremendous difference in how you stroke your putts, even if you don't make any other changes to your mechanics.

about the new mechanics, only then do we graduate to things like alignment at a specific target and green reading. That's just as true for a twenty-handicapper as it is when somebody like Darren Clarke comes to see me.

Speaking of tour players, the rest of this chapter is devoted to the stories of professional players I've worked with over the last few years. These stories start out with the same sort of analysis I described at the beginning of the chapter—a feeling-out phase where I try to figure out just what the player is asking me to do, a stage where I tell my story to them, and then the process they use to incorporate the advice into their games. The added complication with a tour player is that you're dealing with somebody who makes his or her living playing golf. You have to be sensitive to the fact that messing that player up has serious consequences. There have been times when a tour player has asked for a lesson and after ten minutes working together on the practice green, I tell him that it's better we don't work together because he has an approach or technique that isn't what I would choose. One player told me he wanted me to help him putt in a way where he didn't have to have any swing thoughts. I wouldn't know how to go forward with that kind of request, and pushing the method I teach isn't going to do the player any good if he isn't receptive. It will probably just hurt his confidence with the method he's already using. I know how that feels, and I wouldn't want to do that to another professional.

So the stories you're going to read here are all about players who started out receptive to making some kind of improvement to their stroke. When I first get started with a tour player, I'm always fascinated by the relationship between what that player says about his or her stroke and what is actually happening. I find that it works in cycles. When a player is putting well, he seems to have a good understanding about what is really going on with his stroke. Then, when he starts to struggle, things can go one of two ways. Guys with a great grasp of the fundamentals—somebody like Brad Faxon, say—can diagnose the problem and make the necessary adjustments. But sometimes, even the best putters can't "see" the problem themselves. That's where I come in. I'm either helping players make fundamental changes to putt better, or I'm acting as a second set of eyes to confirm that some of their fundamentals are out of whack.

Read through this collection of stories and I'm sure you'll recognize some of your own putting issues. The advice I gave Jay Haas about his grip certainly applies to your game, too, even though you might not be standing over an $85,000 putt. Darren Clarke had his putting grip down in the fingers, just like dozens of amateurs I've seen. When I tell these stories to the twenty-handicappers I teach, they're really encouraged. Putting really is the most democratic skill in golf, and that's what makes it so fun to teach. I couldn't teach you how to hit a 320-yard tee shot like Tiger Woods does. Heck, I can't even hit one of those myself. But anybody can learn to roll the ball well, and it's liberating to know that players at every level struggle with the same faults.

JAY HAAS

My association with Jay really came from being in the right place at the right time. I was having dinner at my friend Dillard Pruitt's house in April 2001. Jay, who is married to Dillard's sister and lives across town from him in Greenville, South Carolina, happened to come by while I was over. We got to talking a little bit about putting, and Jay told me about some of the problems he was having.

We went outside, and Jay made some putting strokes with a 6-iron. I could see right away that some of his fundamentals were off and keeping him from hitting consistently solid putts. He rocked his shoulders instead of turning them, and he shifted the grip back in his backswing instead of getting the putterhead moving. That first night, the only thing I said to him was that he needed to work on turning his shoulders instead of rocking them. He went on his way, and worked on that on his own on the practice green. I heard from him a week later, on the phone, and he said he was feeling a lot better over his putts.

Believe it or not, our relationship actually developed that way, over the phone, without me even working with him in person. We'd talk about the putting stroke, and he'd make a few changes here and there. We first talked in April, and I didn't actually watch him hit putts on the practice green until July. It's a testament to how good Jay is that he was able to get significantly better that way.

What Jay was going through is really common for talented players who haven't had a lot of instruction over the years. He is basically a natural and a hard worker, and he visited with a teacher only for his full swing or when something was broken and he couldn't fix it. I don't think he ever thought about putting mechanics his entire career, and I think his whole game was deteriorating because he was losing confidence in his putting. You really put a tremendous amount of pressure on your driving and iron play when you don't feel like you're going to make putts, and it's easy for your whole game to spiral out of control when that happens. Jay figured he should do something about that, especially with the Champions Tour coming up soon. He was just looking for some logic that he could apply to his putting game. He needed a little bit of direction and some basics that made sense to him. The message I was telling him was pretty simple, too. Then, he could go watch Tiger Woods and Brad Faxon and say, hey, this is what they do.

We started by addressing his grip, turning his left hand from a weak position to a neutral position, and adjusting his setup so that his elbows were softer and more to his sides. We talked a lot about the fundamentals of swinging the club on plane, and how that creates an arc with the putter as much as it does with an iron. The final piece of the puzzle was for him to get his shoulders working around his spine, not tilting back and forth. In this whole process, his goal was to get his ball rolling end over end. Instead of letting his shoulders move up and down like a seesaw in the stroke, I wanted him to

By improving his putting consistency, Jay Haas earned more than $2 million in both 2003 and 2004—the first two times in his twenty-eight-year career that he broke the $1 million mark in earnings.

focus on getting his left shoulder to feel low at address and stay level during the stroke. The next thing we wanted to do was to get him feeling *softer* over his putts. He had a really rigid setup through his legs, and his arms were pretty tense. I wanted him to feel taller in his upper body at address, tilted more from the hips and with a more athletic flex in his knees. Instead of tightening his arms, I wanted him to get them to feel softer and more connected to his body. For him, the feel was almost that his elbows were in front of his body at address, instead of stiff and off to the sides. Then, with the slight shoulder turn on the backswing, he'd feel like the putting stroke was one fluid movement, not a disconnected series of mechanical moves.

Jay's tendency was to really shift the grip end of the putter back on the backswing, which created a lot of extra wrist action in his swing and sucked the energy out of the putterhead end of the club. He had to work pretty hard to hit putts solid, and even harder to get the ball moving on long putts. By turning his shoulders and letting the putter work on an arc, he immediately started getting more consistent results with a lot less effort, and the difference between a really hot putting week—like the one he had at the 2003 Bob Hope, when he shot 28 under par and finished second—and an average week wasn't as great. The toughest part for Jay now is knowing what great putting feels like. He wants to stay there all the time.

DARREN CLARKE

Darren and I finally met at the PGA Championship in 2004, after I had been hearing from Jay Haas for a year that Darren was interested in a lesson. Darren's a great guy to deal with because he really wants to get better and he is willing to commit himself to what you teach him. I think he also knew that his ball-striking was good enough to compete with anybody in the world. It was only some putting and short-game stuff that was keeping him from contending for and winning major championships.

I liked a lot of what Darren did with his putting stroke—it had a nice swing on a good arc—but we needed to do some work on his grip. He tended to let the handle of the putter move down into his fingers, like a full-swing grip. Then, he'd let his shoulders rock a little bit, and the face of his putter would open and lift through impact, instead of releasing and staying low. Most of what I did was remind him to keep the grip in the lifeline of his left hand and to finish low. I also wanted him to feel like his left elbow stayed soft and close to his left side throughout the stroke, so he could get the putter swinging instead of rocking his shoulders through to the finish.

Of course, we all like to go back to what feels good—but that's not necessarily what is fundamentally correct. Now, when Darren struggles with his putter, it's because he lets his right shoulder work

Darren Clarke made some changes to his putting stroke and short game before the 2004 PGA and went out and led the tournament after the first round. He's ready to make the next step and win a major.

up and not around on the backswing. If it were a full swing, you could say he'd almost be coming over the top of the putt. That causes him to either hit a pull, or block it a little bit in an attempt to save it. All it takes is a little reminder to get his left shoulder working toward his chin, and all of a sudden his path is back to perfect and he has putting rounds like he did on Thursday at Whistling Straits. The next step is working on consistency in his setup, so he can have more good weeks.

I can't emphasize enough that you have to constantly monitor your setup and grip fundamentals. Guys like Darren hit dozens of practice putts every day, and they still can let ball position drift too far forward, or get the shoulders rocking instead of pivoting around the spine. I like to use a mirror or video to check my own setup, and I recommend you do the same. You could possibly be making some significant changes to your setup and stroke if you embrace what I'm talking about in this book. Some of the changes will feel strange, and it will be easy—and tempting—to drift back into old habits. Try not to let that happen.

PETER JACOBSEN

I've had a lot of fun working with Peter Jacobsen because it turns out that we have a lot more in common than I would have expected. The first time we worked together was the weekend of the San Diego tournament in 2003. Peter missed the cut there playing two days with Jay, and after hearing about what Jay had been working on with his putting, he called me on Friday night to see if he could come and spend the day Saturday.

Peter works on his full swing with Jim Hardy, and Jim has definitely been emphasizing a one-plane, swing-around-your-body move to Peter for his full swing. It was interesting, then, to see that Peter came to me trying to swing his putter square-to-square, straight back

Peter Jacobsen has been one of my favorite players to work with over the years. Not only was he nice enough to give me some credit when he won in Hartford in 2003—at the age of fifty—he also introduced me to Jim Hardy.

and straight through. It ran counter to what he was trying to do in his full swing, and it also led to him having some really inconsistent putting weeks. He had his shaft leaned to the right at address, and he flipped his wrists pretty significantly through impact. It's safe to say that his putting was keeping him out of the winner's circle at this point—even though he was hitting the ball as well as he ever had.

Before we even did any work on his stroke, Peter was so encouraged by the idea that he could swing his putter around his body, on an arc, just like he did in his full swing. We added loft to his putter right away, and his hands immediately went into a more neutral position, with the shaft ninety degrees at address.

Peter has dedicated a tremendous amount of effort to changing his stroke, and he's really starting to see benefits from it. He won on the regular tour as a senior, in Hartford in 2003, and he's had a great record in senior events, including multiple major championship wins. What really impresses me about him is that he's such a good ball-striker that he didn't have to improve his putting that much to see drastic improvement in his results, but he still spent the time to get the most out of his new stroke. Peter has really had a tremendous career, and most of that success came because of how well he hit it. Now he's competitive on the PGA Tour because of how he can putt, and he's a force on the Champions Tour because of it. I always get a thrill out of seeing how happy a player can be about making more putts—whether that player is a professional or a beginner. It's also nice to see a guy go out and make putts that earn him some big paychecks, like Peter has.

Peter was also instrumental in introducing me to Jim Hardy. I've been able to share my short-game ideas with Jim, and he's been helping me with my full swing. I think Jim and I teach the same kind of information, just at different ends of the swing spectrum. I've never felt so good about how I hit it, and I hope I've been able to help Jim a little bit with his stroke. I know having received Jim's blessing for the techniques I share has been a big encouragement to me. Thanks to Jim, I've got a much clearer understanding of how the golf swing works and how the full swing and what I teach work together. I'm also happy that Jim and Peter have the information they need to work on Peter's game independent of me and have great success.

CRAIG STADLER

Of all the tour players I've worked with, Craig came to me in the worst shape, by far. You've read a lot up to this point about the swing arc I teach. Craig's putting stroke actually arced the opposite way, from outside the target line to outside the target line. He certainly wasn't doing it on purpose. I had seen enough of him winning tournaments on television over the years to know he wasn't doing that when he was making all those putts at Augusta. It was just something that had developed over time—probably from overcooking some other kind of tip or stroke correction.

When I talked to him the first time, after the West Coast swing in 2003, he told me he was literally four-putting, and he was worried it might be mental. He would go hit putts on the practice green with this opposite-curving stroke and do okay with it, then play a tournament round and putt it thirty-eight or forty times. I watched him hit four or five putts and immediately told him I had great news. It wasn't mental, and he didn't have the yips. His stroke was terrible. I don't have any doubt that he was liberated by the knowledge that he could fix a big-time mechanical flaw and become a great player again.

A big factor for Craig in getting better so quickly was that he had putted the way I teach for most of his career. The problems had only crept in recently. We first talked about why the putterhead needs to swing on plane, and the arc that it creates. I then attached a pen laser from the Scotty Cameron putting studio to his shaft to give him a visual idea of where his stroke was traveling. When the laser is pointed straight down the shaft and the putter is swinging on plane, the laser light will travel straight along the target line. This visual allowed Craig to immediately grasp what his stroke needed to do and to adapt quickly to the proper feels. For him, the laser went from making a U-shape to a nice straight line.

Craig Stadler is a testament to the fact that you don't need to use a conventional putting grip to take advantage of the techniques I teach. His stroke looks great, and he's winning everything on the Champions Tour.

The fixes were pretty simple. He got his shoulders working around his spine and his forearms rotating, and he really just clicked in to what he used to do. Craig went to the claw grip shortly after we worked together, not because I suggested it, but because it really helped him turn his shoulders and keep the putter on plane. I'm all for anything that helps you make a nice swing arc and keep the putter on plane.

Believe it or not, that one visit—and a quick checkup at the Masters three weeks later—are the only visits Craig and I have had. I can't take credit for all the wins he's had on the Champions Tour since then, but I know he's swinging his putter completely differently now than he was before. In 2004, he was first in birdies, scoring and money on the Champions Tour, and third in putting.

ROCCO MEDIATE

Rocco's story is an interesting one. He played on tour for a long time with a long putter, not so much because of his stroke, but because of his back. He was a below-average putter, but his back wouldn't let him spend much time on the practice green if he had to do it while bent over a standard-length putter. So he soldiered along with the long putter, having mixed success—and the good weeks almost always came because of how he was hitting the ball, not how he was putting it.

We hooked up early in 2005 because his back felt better and he wanted to get back to a conventional putter, but this time, he wanted to get some direction about how to roll the ball better. Working with Rocco has been a lot of fun because what I'm sharing with him is stuff he's really hearing for the first time. His putting stroke with the conventional putter was really different from what I teach—handsy, with the grip end shifting a lot back and forth in the stroke. The result for him was something really mechanical-feeling, which is pretty much the opposite of his full-swing game. He's a graceful, fluid player with his long clubs, and I wanted to get some of that fluidness and athleticism into his putting game.

We started by making some big changes to his putter, making it thirty-six inches long instead of thirty-four, flattening the lie angle and giving it more loft. We got his hands on the putter with a reverse overlap grip, and his left hand in a position where it would match the way it hangs naturally—neutral instead of weak. Next, we turned his elbows more toward his sides, so they were pointing to his hips. This allowed his forearms and the putter shaft to align. These changes—and having him get the putterhead moving back first instead of the grip end—have given him an enthusiasm about putting that he's never had before. He's really swinging his arms now and letting them flow like they do in his long game. Although he's still learning his new stroke, he's seen flashes of how well he can really putt, and I think he's excited. He called the 67 he shot in the first round at the 2005 U.S. Open one of the best putting rounds of his life. The best part for him—and for me—is that he's just getting started.

PAUL MCGINLEY

Paul and Darren Clarke are buddies, and my association with both of them came from a generous recommendation from Butch Harmon. He's been great to work with because he's so dedicated, going through a lot of effort to visit me in Scottsdale when he feels like he needs some work. Paul swings very "around," with a flatter swing plane, and what I teach in putting and the short game really goes with the way Paul hits the golf ball.

A big piece of his putting is that he's a fast-twitch muscle kind of guy. He likes to feel a very aggressive hit on the ball. A big key for him is to keep his right elbow not only soft but close to his right side on the takeaway, versus swinging away and down the target line. When he keeps his right elbow soft like that, it makes the putterhead swing first and foremost. For him, it feels soft and wristy in the backswing, but that's not what it looks like in real life. What it does is let him load the putter and then release it on a nice arc. When the grip end floats away on the backswing, he doesn't really swing the clubhead back, and he ends up throwing the putterhead with his wrists to generate enough energy to hit the putt. His release is really different and less consistent that way. He really likes one of the drills

The biggest shot in McGinley's life was the putt he made to win the 2002 Ryder Cup for Europe. Still, he wanted to improve that part of his game, and we've been working on just that—he won the European Tour Championship at the end of 2005.

I'm going to show you in the next chapter—hitting putts with just the right hand, with the left hand touching the right bicep during the stroke. That forces his right elbow to stay close and not float. His right forearm also tended to get high in his address, which caused him to aim to the left. Helping him with that softer right-arm position at address also got his forearms to align with his target.

SHIGEKI MARUYAMA

I gave Shigeki a lesson at the Phoenix Open in 2005 through an interpreter—which wasn't as complicated as I expected it to be. He said he really struggled on putts from ten to fifteen feet that broke just a little bit. For whatever reason, I think I asked a perfect question: When that is happening, what happens on your straight putts? He said he made every one of them. It turns out that he was focusing on the hole during his setup. His eyes were looking back and forth at the hole, instead of at the high point—the point he needed to aim at to get the ball to curve into the hole. If you look at the hole on a breaking putt, your tendency is to hit the ball at the hole. A simple adjustment in his pre-shot routine—getting him to focus on the point he wanted the ball to roll to on a breaking putt instead of at the hole—made all the difference. He didn't even have to change his stroke.

Shigeki Maruyama's putting problem was one common to most players. He was having his last look at the hole, instead of his start line for breaking putts.

TAYLORE KARLE

Taylore is a really talented junior player from Scottsdale who had never really had any guidance when it came to her putting. When we started, her left-hand grip was a little weak, and her shaft leaned back slightly, away from the target. When she was in her address position, she used to hold her elbows out, away from her sides. She tended to make a short backswing, which forced her to really accelerate the putter on the downswing to get enough power.

Taylore is a tremendous learner, and she absorbed what I had to say right away. We strengthened that left-hand grip and got her some forward press, softened her elbows and improved her posture. I also explained the arc to her, and she incorporated the idea into her putting by focusing on the concept of turning her shoulders around her spine. In a short amount of time, Taylore's lag putting got dramatically better, and after four or five months of work, she got tremendously confident over short putts. She turned fifteen last summer and had a great tournament season, winning a handful of AJGA events around the country and setting the thirty-six-hole scoring record to make it to match play at the U.S. Girls Junior. She was rewarded by being named a 2005 AJGA Rolex Junior First Team All-American, along with Morgan Pressel and a handful of other talented junior players. We played a few holes recently, and I'm happy to report that I can still drive it longer than she can—barely.

CHAPTER 8
PUTTING DRILLS

. . . .

I t's one thing to describe a good putting stroke to you. But I'm sure
you're wondering how you're going to take the ideas I've been
talking about here and get them to stick in your own game. We've
talked about feel over and over, and it really is true that you need to
feel the way the putter releases effortlessly when you make the kind of
stroke I've been talking about. That's where the drills in this chapter
come in.

The eight drills I'm going to show you here will not only help you
feel the basics of a good putting stroke, but also help you get back on
track later on, after you've learned the stroke but are going through a
rough patch. I use every one of these drills with the tour players I
teach to help get them locked in. I like them because they travel well.
You're not always going to have a teacher or a reference book with
you to check on your game. Being able to set up your own reference
arc with a yardstick or learning how to use coins to make sure you're
hitting down on your putts is going to help you remember some of
the things we've talked about in this book when you're on the course.

One other thing to keep in mind when you're trying these drills—
or even just hitting practice putts on the putting green—is that
you've got to change up the holes you're hitting to. Anybody can
stand over the same eight- or ten-footer and, with enough practice,

learn how to shake putts in the hole even with a bad stroke. What you're trying to do with these drills and your putting practice is to develop touch and feel over a variety of putting situations. You're building touch and feel into your new stroke just by changing the hole you hit to and adjusting to a variety of different breaks. I don't like to hit any more than eight or ten putts to the same target when I'm practicing or warming up before a round. I'll move to a different spot and hit putts with a different break, even if it's to the same hole. In the five or ten minutes on the practice green right before a tournament round, I'll even hit some twenty-, thirty- and forty-footers with no target in mind, just to get a feel for the speed of the green and the weight of the clubhead. Just doing that will help your rhythm and feel tremendously.

PUTT WITH ONE HAND

Many players who struggle with the putter are struggling because of too much tension in the upper body. The stroke starts to look like a stiff, full-body jab. The goal is to get that player to feel that the energy in the putting stroke comes from the head end of the putter, not the grip end. Start by carefully setting your right-hand grip and getting into a conventional putting stance. Cross your left arm on your chest so that your hand is on the front of your right bicep. Next, make a half-dozen practice strokes using just the right hand. Feel the weight of the putterhead and how it wants to swing itself without too much body movement to help it. With the left hand on your right bicep, you can feel how little it moves in a good stroke. In fact, most of the movement comes from below the elbows. The weight of the putterhead will help you rotate your forearm on the downswing as well—this is what you want, as opposed to breaking the wrist to flip at the ball.

Next, change to your left-hand grip and make some practice

swings with just that hand, crossing the right arm over the chest. Again, the stroke comes from forearm rotation, not from wrist movement. Once you feel the weight of the clubhead—and with only one hand on the putter, you'll really start to feel it—you'll sense how the putter wants to arc open on the backswing and close after impact with no extra hand movement.

After eight or ten putts each with the right and left hands, make your standard putting grip and hit five putts, keeping in mind how each hand moved independently through the stroke when it was holding the club by itself. You should immediately sense how easily they work together, supporting the rotation of the forearms. You don't have to grip the putter tightly or manipulate the club open or closed to get it to work. The weight of the club wants to help you do what you're supposed to do.

(LEFT) By swinging with just your right hand, you're much more sensitive to the weight of the putterhead.
(RIGHT) This one-handed grip also reinforces the idea that most of the movement in the putting stroke happens from the elbows down.

(ABOVE LEFT) Once you've hit putts with your right hand, switch around and hit some using just your left hand. Keep that feeling of rotating the forearm to make the stroke, not flipping the wrist.

(ABOVE RIGHT) You'll notice that the easiest way to hit putts with one hand is to let the putter follow the arc, with the face opening like it is here. You can generate a tremendous amount of energy without much effort.

(LEFT) I haven't done much at all with my arms, and the putterhead has released nicely and the ball is on its way. Notice how quiet my lower body has stayed.

STROKE REFERENCE

Everyone expects me to pull out some elaborate training aid for players to work on their strokes with, but my props are pretty simple. You
can practice the stroke I teach with just an aluminum yardstick and
three tees. The aluminum yardstick has just enough flex that it can
bend in a slight curve. Balance the yardstick on its edge and stick a
tee in the green at the center of the yardstick on the inside edge.
Then, curve each end toward you slightly and stick tees in the
ground at the outside edge of the yardstick to support the curve.
The curve in the yardstick you've created with the tees stuck in the
ground should be pretty gentle, having only pulled in each end
about an inch and a half from the center. Now, you have a track to
guide your putter for both practice strokes and real putts.

I like to use this track three different ways. The first way is to put
the ball on the inside of the curve, and use the yardstick as a simple
reference line. Then, you can hit practice putts with this visual cue re-
minding you of the right arc.

By moving closer to the yardstick and placing the heel of your
putter on the outside of it, right up against the metal, you can actually use the yardstick as a physical guide for the stroke. Make a
stroke with the heel of the putter right alongside the metal during
the entire stroke and you'll really feel the swing arc.

The third way to use it is to place your putter on the top edge of
the yardstick, with the aiming line on the top edge of the putter in
line with the top edge of the yardstick. Then you can make more practice strokes while keeping the line on the top of the putter centered
on the top edge of the yardstick. Having a visual reference really
makes a difference when you're trying to develop—or maintain—your
putting stroke.

I've seen some "putting arc" training aids for sale in golf shops
and on infomercials. These will work just fine, but bending your own
yardstick is cheaper and easier to do. The yardstick will also hide

(ABOVE LEFT AND RIGHT) After creating the guide with a yardstick and three tees, start by using it to the outside of your target line. (LEFT) Let the putter follow the arc back and through, making sure to set the ball up just inside the leading edge of the arc so that it can clear it on the way to the hole.

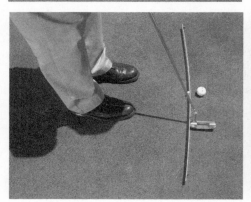

(ABOVE LEFT) By moving forward and hitting putts from the other side of the arc, you can physically use the metal of the yardstick to guide your stroke.
(ABOVE RIGHT) Slide the putter along the metal on the way back and through and you'll get a great feel for the arc.

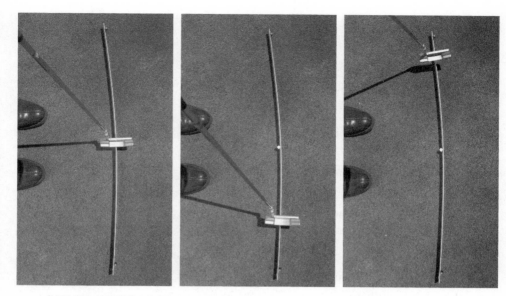

(LEFT AND CENTER) A final way to check your path is to make some swings with the putter on top of the arc guide. Don't let the guide drift toward the heel end of the putter—which it will do if you try to take the putter straight back.
(RIGHT) As you go through the downswing, let the putter slide along the top of the guide and then release away from the metal at the end of the stroke.

away in your golf bag without taking up too much room. I use this set of drills myself when I've been away from tournament action for a couple of weeks, just to sharpen my putting path.

MOVE THE COINS

If you've always used a putter without enough loft, you're probably scooping your hands and breaking your wrists through impact. Bending the putter to get enough loft on it sometimes solves the problem right away. I remember visiting with John Daly once, when he was really struggling with his putting. I took a look at his putter and saw that it had two degrees of loft on it. Knowing that John didn't want to hear any technical advice, I told his caddie about it, and the caddie went out and bent the putter to about five degrees of loft. John went out and won the next week because he felt better over the ball, even if he didn't know why.

If you still have some remnants of that scoop in your stroke after checking your loft, try this coin drill and you'll erase it pretty quickly. Make a stack of two quarters and a penny, and put it an inch behind your ball, right on the target line. Three inches in front of the ball, make a stack of two dimes, again right on the target line. Your putting stroke should cause the putter to miss the stack of coins behind the ball, then hit the stack of coins in front of the ball, after you've hit the putt.

This drill will immediately get you hitting down on your putts instead of scooping them, and you'll start maintaining the forward shaft angle and holding the angle of your right wrist through impact. It might feel a little awkward at first, but you'll get over that when you see how much more true your putts roll. The feeling at impact should be much more solid, and it will immediately take a lot less effort to get your ball to roll out.

(TOP) Place a stack of two quarters and a penny one inch behind the ball, along the target line, and a stack of two dimes three inches in front of the ball, also on the target line. Avoid the stack of coins on the backswing and the beginning of the downswing. (BOTTOM) On the downswing, avoid the stack of coins behind the ball, and try to push the stack of coins in front of the ball after making contact with your putt.

CHECKING THE PUTTING PLANE

Plane is a difficult thing to check when you're hitting putts by your-self, but with a simple assist from a friend, you can check it two ways. First, have your friend crouch to the side of you, straddling the tar-get line. Ask him or her to hold a club parallel to the target line, halfway up between the putterhead and the bottom of the grip, against the back of the shaft of your putter. Then, hit some practice putts. Your putter should slide along the shaft without the pressure changing. If it leaves the shaft or pushes hard against it, you will be able to instantly feel your tendency to leave the swing plane. This process helps you learn what "plane" looks like, and how it works in conjunction with swing path to produce a pure stroke.

By holding a guide club parallel to the target line, halfway between the clubhead and grip, and just behind and gently against the shaft of my student's putter, I can make sure he keeps his putter on a nice plane. If his putter leaves my shaft or pushes it out of place, his stroke is moving off the desired plane.

Another way to use a club as a check is to have your friend hold it along the target line, just above your putterhead. Your goal is to make stroke while keeping the putter low to the ground and under your friend's club. It forces you to make a shoulder turn and swing on the arc, not rock the shoulders up and down and lift the putter.

Here, I'm holding a club shaft slightly above my student's clubhead, along the target line. He makes practice strokes with my club there, making sure to keep his stroke low to the ground. This drill helps promote an arc and shoulder turn, instead of a shoulder rock.

HIT TO THE HAND

Practice your normal stroke and allow your friend to stop your through swing just after impact. It will be easy for both of you to tell if you have released the hand too early and lost your slight forward shaft lean through the strike on the ball. Now hit a few putts with this drill and feel how solid a good stroke is supposed to be. This drill will also help you find your instinct for the appropriate length backswing.

The idea here is to have your friend's hand cause the end of your stroke. You will learn from how your shaft is leaning at this point. If the putterhead is way ahead of the grip when the shaft hits your friend's hand, you have released or flipped the clubhead too early. If you reach your friend's hand with the shaft still near vertical, you will have maintained your right wrist angle as well as released your right elbow properly through impact. This should create the perfect feel for the proper way to end a great stroke—low, short and through the ball. Mr. Lanning called this "dead strength."

From the setup position, I put my hand just in front of my student's putter-shaft, three inches past where impact would be. I'm trying to get him to think about accelerating through impact.

Your goal here is to hit your shaft squarely into the hand—which means the shaft came through impact at ninety degrees or leaned a little bit forward, toward the target. If you flip your hands, the bottom end of the puttershaft will hit the hand first and you'll hit the ball with a glancing blow.

NARROW YOUR FOCUS

I always like to see practice greens that have the small, two-inch-wide practice holes—they're a great way to focus your concentration on a smaller target. That way, when you go out onto the course, the regular four-inch hole looks huge. Most places don't have those holes cut into the practice green, but you can improvise with a couple of tees. Just stick the tees lightly in the grass a half inch inside each edge of the cup. Essentially, you're creating a set of mini-goalposts to hit putts through. I like to put the tees in and set up for a six- or seven-footer without any break, and practice just rolling putts through the goal posts. It sounds simple, but when you try it, you'll notice how much more acutely you focus. Instead of picking a nebulous, large target, you're almost picking blades of grass to roll the ball over. Again, it makes putting into the standard holes seem easy in comparison.

THE PRE-ROUND DRILL

The first few drills I've described here are great for practice days when you've got a lot of time and a pile of balls. But what do you do before an important round of golf to get yourself mentally and physically prepared? When I get to the golf course, I start out on the practice green, hitting putts for twenty minutes or so to get myself into the "golf" mindset. After that, I go to the practice range and proceed with my normal full-swing warm-up until about ten minutes before my tee time. Then I walk back to the practice green (which is almost always near the first tee) and spend five minutes trying to accomplish three very distinct goals. First, I want to find the one or two swing thoughts that I'm going to go with in my putting for the day. It could be something left over from the day before, when I had a good round, or something I discovered during my preliminary practice session. Once I've got that locked in, I hit about a dozen long putts across the green, to no particular target. I don't care where the ball is going so much as I want to feel good rhythm and solid contact. After those putts, which really help me refine my sense of the overall speed of the greens, the last thing I want to do before I go play is reinforce the feel of actually making putts. I'll pick a practice hole and work my way around it, sinking two- and three-footers. I always make sure to make three putts in a row before I actually walk to the tee, to make sure I'm heading into action with a positive feeling.

OFF-SEASON PRACTICE

If you aren't lucky enough to live in a year-round golf place like Arizona, what do you do to keep your putting stroke sharp in the winter? Before moving out here a couple of years ago, I spent my winters in Missouri, so I had to figure out a way to do just that. I bought one of those fake-turf putting mats—mine was about twelve feet long—and spent the winter doing two things. First, I set up in front of a full-length mirror and really scrutinized my grip, stance and posture. It really makes you learn what a good setup looks like—something that will help you diagnose and fix stroke problems out on the course. It's tough to use a mirror to actually watch your own stroke—mostly because your attention should be on the ball, and you'd be watching from a funny angle—but you can get what you need by checking the setup. Once you've done that, just practice stroking straight putts on the mat or a piece of flat carpet. The speed of the surface doesn't really matter. You're just trying to translate that setup work into actually aiming yourself over a putt. One winter in Missouri, I just wore that putting mat out, stroking twelve-footer after twelve-footer. I can remember coming out for my first event in the spring, in Florida, and the first putt I saw on the first hole was exactly the same length as the one I had been hitting all winter. All the repetition in the basement had really helped me sharpen my ability to set up square to my target and make a pressure-free stroke without worrying about the consequences. It was just another putt on the fake green in my basement.

THE YIPS

I want to address one more thing here before we finish up. A lot of players ask me about the yips—what they are, and if you can fix them. I try not to think about them as a player, but as a teacher, they're a fact of life. From what I can figure, the yips come from a subconscious effort to try to correct an error in the stroke. For example, your brain subconsciously knows that you're aimed wrong on a two-footer, and tries to short circuit your muscles to correct it. Have that happen more than a few times and it'll wreck your confidence. It's certainly hard to get rid of totally. I'm not going to say it's never a mental thing, or never a nervous thing, but I'll say that it's usually some kind of flaw in the stroke itself that leads up to it. I think a player who strokes it better or different has a good chance to overcome it. Better technique leads to more consistent contact, which will help anyone's confidence increase.

The players I've seen who've suffered from the yips have had the most success beating them by switching to a less-conventional method like a claw grip, belly putter or long putter. That approach doesn't so much "fix" the problem as it does work around it. That's completely okay with me—I'm for anything that makes you feel more comfortable on the green, as long as the fundamentals are good. And you can use a claw grip, left-hand-low grip or even a belly putter and use the techniques I've been talking about in this book. Mostly you've got to be willing to make some changes and experiment to try to fix the problem. Stubbornly doing the same things and missing short putt after short putt isn't going to do anything but permanently burn out your confidence.

CHAPTER 9
QUICK REFERENCE GUIDE

. . . .

You've gone through the book and made some changes to your putting stroke. That's great—but it's just the first step. If golf was as simple as learning a skill and then repeating it over and over again, professional golf would be really boring to watch, with 125 guys shooting 63 every day. Golf—and putting—is about making adjustments. We aren't machines, and fundamentals get out of whack for even the best players. That's why I have mostly ongoing relationships with tour players, not just one-time fix sessions.

The moral of this story is that you shouldn't get discouraged if you go through some rough patches with your new putting stroke. It happens to the best players, and the only way out of it is to go back to the fundamentals and rebuild your confidence. This quick reference guide will help you do that. It's designed to remind you of the things we've talked about and worked on in this book, and to help you get back on track if you start to struggle.

The putting stroke is pretty simple and straightforward. But it's also precise. Hit a tee shot with a slightly open face on your driver and you might miss in the light rough on the right. Hit a putt that way and you might miss a big five-footer to win a match. The good news is, by checking your fundamentals regularly and sticking to the basics, you can maintain your stroke and avoid slumps. When I haven't been playing a lot of golf and need to get back into tournament putting form, I essentially start from the beginning and go over the elements on this checklist, point by point, to rebuild my feel. It really is true that an hour invested on the practice green once or twice a month during your own golf season can pay bigger dividends than time spent working on any other part of your game. That's because solid, consistent putting can bail you out during a sketchy ball-striking day—and turn a good ball-striking day into a great scoring round.

Grip

- The putter grip should run up the lifelines, not down across the first joints of the fingers.
- In a good putting grip, the shaft runs in a line parallel to the forearms—not under them as it would for a full shot.
- I recommend the reverse overlap grip, where the index finger of the left hand extends over the top of the fingers of the right hand.
- Grip pressure should be light, emphasizing feel in the fingertips— the part of your body responsible for touch.
- Both thumbs should be parallel, on top of the shaft. This sets the hands up parallel to each other and square to the target line at address.
- If you decide to use a nonconventional grip (cross-handed, claw), it is still important to set the hands so that the top of the forearms are square to the target line.

Stance

- A narrow stance is the most natural—you'd stand that way if we were having a conversation.
- Tilt from the hips, don't slouch the shoulders.
- Weight should be balanced across your feet from left to right and front to back.

Setup

- I like a square setup, with the shoulders, hips, knees and feet square to the target line.
- It's okay to set up with the feet a little open to the line as long as the primary alignment—the top of the forearms—stays square to the target line.
- The putterface should be at the center of your stance, with the ball just ahead of that.
- The shoulders and elbows should be relaxed and soft. The elbows should be soft and resting against your sides, not stiff and extended.
- The shaft should be at ninety degrees at address, or leaning a little bit toward the target. It's hard to hit the ball solid if you start with the shaft leaning back.
- Hold the putter in your dominant hand and use your dominant eye first when getting into your setup position. You will align yourself more accurately to the target.

Stroke

- The stroke comes from the shoulders turning around your spine, not the rocking of the shoulders up and down.
- The stroke is simple—the right elbow folds and the left arm extends, and then the right arm extends while the left folds.
- The putterhead should look like it is opening on the backswing and closing through impact, but this isn't something you do by flipping or turning your hands. It happens with shoulder turn and a slight forearm rotation.

Swing Thoughts

- Feel the swing of the putterhead in the takeaway by allowing the right elbow to soften.
- Release the tension in your shoulders before you make a practice stroke. Tense shoulders destroy feel.

- Release the putter by extending your right elbow rotating the forearms, not by flipping your wrists.
- Allow your shoulders to work around your spine tilt, not against it.

PUTTING PROBLEMS

Pulls

- Check your ball position. A pull can come from the ball being too far forward in your stance—where the natural arc of the stroke sends the ball left.
- Make sure the right forearm isn't higher than the left in your setup. This can be caused by a too-weak grip (hands turned toward the target) or a shoulder tilt (right shoulder higher than left).
- A closed stance (feet, hips, shoulders turned to the right of the target line) can actually cause a pull. You'll subconsciously yank the putter back to the left during the stroke to compensate for the right alignment.
- A too-long putter can cause you to stand too far from the ball, which lifts the toe of the putter and causes you to aim left.
- A putter with a too-upright lie angle will cause you to aim left.

Pushes

- Rotate the shoulders, don't rock them. Rocking causes the putter to go back closed and come through open, which causes the push.
- Make sure the left forearm isn't higher than the right. This can be caused by a strong grip (hands turned away from the target) or too much shoulder tilt (left shoulder higher than right).
- Stiff elbows and shoulders will promote a push—the clubhead can't release with all the tension.

- Ball position too far back can cause a push, but it's uncommon for players to set up with the ball back.
- A putter with a too-flat lie angle will cause you to aim right.

Feel

- A tight grip with the handle deep in the fingers takes the sensitive fingertips out of the stroke—a mistake. Keep the grip in the lifeline, with the fingertips more on the grip than the palms.
- Losing the mix of shoulder turn and arm swing is devastating to feel. A stiff, shoulders-only swing doesn't work well. You wouldn't toss something underhanded with just a shoulder turn. Feel comes from a flowing mix of shoulder turn, arm swing and forearm rotation.

Distance Control

- The best way to improve distance control is to improve your fundamentals. If you hit it solid, you'll have an incredibly natural sense for how far it will go.
- Grain impacts speed on all greens, not just those with Bermuda grass. On bentgrass greens, look for the shine. If, from behind your ball, the grass looks dark and almost shadowed, you're hitting into the grain and need to give it more speed. If the grass looks shiny, you're with the grain and the putt will be faster.

Green Reading

- Walk from your approach shot to the green with your eyes open—it gives you an overall feel for the tilt of the green.
- Examine your putt first from behind the ball, then from behind the hole and then from the low side of the break halfway between the ball and the hole.
- Most amateurs drastically underestimate the amount of break. If in doubt, play more break, especially on intermediate length putts (fifteen to twenty-five feet)

- Be conscious of aiming at your target—the apex of the break—and not cheating your aim toward the hole.
- Grain will impact your read most dramatically on fast downhill and sidehill putts.

Equipment

- Putters with toe-hang (perimeter weighting that causes the toe to drop when the shaft is balanced on your finger) work with the stroke I teach. Face-balanced putters do not work as well—they're designed for a straight-back-straight-through stroke.
- Putter fit is just as important as fit in the other clubs in your bag. A putter that is too short, too tall, or too upright will cause you to have to make compensations in your stroke.
- Most off-the-rack putters are too short (thirty-two inches instead of thirty-four or thirty-six), too upright (seventy-one degrees of lie angle instead of sixty-nine) and don't have enough loft (three degrees instead of five). Keep this in mind, and be prepared to have your putter bent to suit your new stroke. I most often fit people at thirty-five inches, sixty-eight degrees of lie angle, and five degrees of loft.
- A thinner grip enhances your feel for the putterhead.
- The most important cosmetic element about your putter is the way its alignment looks at address. You want a putter that clearly looks square when you set up over the ball. If a putter looks open or closed (or is actually open or closed) to the target line at address, you will struggle with consistency.

ACKNOWLEDGMENTS

. . . .

Creating *The Art of Putting* was certainly a team effort. Matthew Rudy did a great job with my words, and J.D. Cuban's photographs are awesome. My agent, Scott Waxman, deserves a lot of credit for putting it all together, and Brendan Cahill and Patrick Mulligan at Gotham Books were great to work with.

Developing Stan Utley the player and teacher was a team effort, too. I want to say thanks to my dad, Frank Utley, who became a golf fanatic when I was ten years old. He was my first coach, and he taught me how to think, both on the golf course and off. My mom, Ruby, taught me patience and positive thinking. My brother John has been a best friend forever and is now the ultimate business associate.

I also owe a lot to a lady named Rhoda Luna, who taught me great fundamentals when I was ten years old. Bob Paris was the best player at the club when I was a kid, and more importantly, was always a perfect gentleman and a person a kid could look up to. Craig Linson, John Richards, Gates Paris and I became a foursome of golfers and buddies from the time I moved to West Plains all the way through high school. We played thousands of matches together, and I remember those times as some of the best in my life.

Ken Lanning has been the most dominant figure in my golf life. The more I learn over the years, the more I realize that the things

Mr. Lanning told me when I was a teenager were right. Along that line, Mr. Lanning and Jim Tom Blair explained the putting stroke to me, and made all this possible. Rich Poe gave me a golf scholarship at the University of Missouri, and was a great mentor and friend. Craig Harrison was the first teacher I had after school, and was there for my first PGA Tour win. He really pushed me to work hard, and I owe him a lot for that. Other teachers who have been positive influences on me are Fred Griffin, Rob Akins and Jim Hardy. I also want to thank David Cook and Rick McGuire for their mental and spiritual coaching.

Ed Roberson took a big risk on a young pro, sponsoring me when nobody else was knocking down my door. He'll never realize how important he was to my development, giving me the ability to make some choices at the start of my career. Buddy Henry gave me a sponsor's exemption into his PGA Tour event in Chattanooga. I won that week, and it changed my life.

I would like to mention Dillard Pruitt, Fred Wadsworth and Brandel Chamblee as well. These guys were my running buddies when I turned pro. We traveled the mini-tours together, played practice rounds together, ate a ton of bad food and slept in a lot of lousy hotel rooms. We'll always be lifelong friends.

I have to thank my wife, Elayna, more than anyone. She's been my partner, my wife, my coach and my best friend. I certainly couldn't have had the career I've had without her help.

I also want to acknowledge my Lord and Savior—the giver of great gifts, who has given me the passion to encourage others not just to know Him, but to know and understand golf a little bit better.

The
LEARNING CURVE
By Stan Utley

As I was writing this book and working with the guys on Tour, it became apparent that I needed a tool to help my students feel what I was teaching. I began working with EyeLine Golf to develop a guide that would visually and physically demonstrate the fundamentals of the "on plane" stroke. The finished product is called the Learning Curve.

Using this tool whenever you practice will have you making a more natural stroke in just a few sessions. Use it on the putting green or in your home. Your touch will improve as you begin to let your hands and arms make the stroke.

This is a great game,
Stan Utley

Includes a full length instructional  DVD VIDEO™

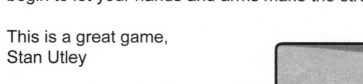

To order:
Call **800.969.3764**
or visit **www.eyelinegolf.com**